Roberto Lalli delle Malebranche

Waves

Your Presentations Will Transform The World

~

This is the extended version of my book
Presenting For The Revolution

"THERE IS A CANDLE IN YOUR HEART, READY TO BE KINDLED. THERE IS A VOID IN YOUR SOUL, READY TO BE FILLED. YOU FEEL IT, DON'T YOU?"

~ RUMI

"WE MUST LET GO OF THE LIFE WE HAVE PLANNED, SO AS TO ACCEPT THE ONE THAT IS WAITING FOR US."

~ JOSEPH CAMPBELL

MY FRIEND, OUR WORLD IS ON THE BRINK OF DESTRUCTION, AND NO ONE CAN SAVE IT BUT US. WITH DETERMINATION, WITH A SMILE—AND WITH OUR PRESENTATIONS.

IN FACT, OUR PRESENTATIONS ARE A GREAT TOOL TO TRANSFORM OUR WORLD FOR THE BETTER BECAUSE THEY MIRROR THE FEARS, IDEAS AND DREAMS OF HUMANITY. THAT'S WHY, ONCE WE START TO GO BEYOND MANIPULATION, EASY PROFIT AND SUCCESS AT ANY COST, OUR PRESENTATIONS WILL START TO MAKE A REAL POSITIVE DIFFERENCE FOR OUR AUDIENCE—AND FOR OURSELVES. SLOWLY BUT IRRESISTIBLY, THEY WILL TRANSFORM OUR WORLD INTO A MORE JUST, GREEN AND HUMANE ONE.

IF YOU ACCEPT YOUR MISSION AND BRAVELY START YOUR HERO'S JOURNEY, I PROMISE YOU THAT FROM THIS DAY ON YOU WILL NEVER WALK ALONE AGAIN. YOU WILL REALISE THAT THERE ARE MILLIONS OF US FEELING AND THINKING JUST LIKE YOU AND LONGING JUST LIKE YOU TO SEE THIS WORLD TRANSFORMED.

COME ON, THIS IS THE WAY. A BEAUTIFUL JOURNEY IS WAITING FOR US!

ROBERTO LALLI DELLE MALEBRANCHE

MANNHEIM, 24 JULY 2020

Table of Content ~
What you can expect from this book

Introduction ~ Who we are

"WE HAVE NOT EVEN TO RISK THE ADVENTURE ALONE, FOR THE HEROES OF ALL TIME HAVE GONE BEFORE US."

~ JOSEPH CAMPBELL

WE ARE ALL RELUCTANT HEROES. WE ALL KNOW THAT OUR WORLD IS ACHING UNDER THE TERRIBLE WEIGHT OF INEQUALITY, ENVIRONMENTAL DESTRUCTION AND WARS, BUT WE TRY NOT TO SEE IT, RIGHT?

STUBBORNLY, WE WANT TO BECOME HAPPY IN THE MIDST OF THESE TEARS, CRIES AND DESPERATE PRAYERS ALL AROUND US.

WE HEAR THE CALL OF DESTINY, WE KNOW THAT WE SHOULD ACT, BUT WE DO NOT FIND THE COURAGE TO CONFRONT THE ENORMOUS CHALLENGES AHEAD.

THAT'S NOT SURPRISING, GIVEN THAT OUR PAST AS HUMAN KIND IS NOT VERY ENCOURAGING. THE HISTORY OF MANKIND—OUR HISTORY—IS A STORY WRITTEN WITH THE RED INK OF BLOOD, A STORY ABOUT EXPLOITATION, INEQUALITY AND WARS.

BUT DOES THIS MEAN THAT WE CAN'T TRY TO CHANGE THE COURSE OF OUR HISTORY AND GIVE IT A NEW DIRECTION?

FOLLOW ME FOR A COUPLE OF MINUTES BACK INTO OUR PAST IN ORDER TO FIND AN ANSWER TO THIS QUESTION.

THE FEW VS. THE MANY ~

THE WORLD AS WE KNOW IT TODAY BEGAN TO FORM LONG AGO, BETWEEN 13,000 AND 4,000 YEARS B.C., WHEN GROUPS OF HUNTERS AND GATHERERS, OUR ANCESTORS, BECAME STABLE IN THEIR TERRITORIES AND STARTED TO CULTIVATE FIELDS, RAISE CATTLE AND BUILD TOWNSHIPS TOGETHER.

TODAY WE KNOW THAT EVOLUTION BUILT SPECIAL GENES AND NEURONIC PATTERNS INTO OUR BODIES AND BRAINS IN ORDER TO ACHIEVE EXACTLY THAT: TO GET US TO COOPERATE

WITH OTHER HUMAN BEINGS PERMANENTLY. WHY? BECAUSE HUNTER-GATHERERS WHO BECOME STABLE AND WORK TOGETHER REGULARLY WILL FEED BETTER AND MORE OFTEN AND WILL SURVIVE MORE EASILY—THUS PASSING THEIR GENES ON SUCCESSFULLY.

BUT COOPERATION BECAME THE PRECONDITION TO MUCH MORE THAN SIMPLE SURVIVAL, IT MADE THE MEMBERS OF THESE NEW COMMUNITIES LOOK BEYOND THEIR PERSONAL INTERESTS. YOU SEE, MILITARY TECHNOLOGY, ART, ORGANISED RELIGION, SCIENCE AND SPORTS COULD ONLY DEVELOP THANKS TO THE NEW IDEA OF A COMMON GOOD.

THE EMERGING SPECIALISTS HAD TO BE PAID OUT OF THE SURPLUS CREATED BY THOSE WHO CONTINUED TO CULTIVATE THE FIELDS AND TO HUNT DOWN THE ANIMALS, AND THESE PEASANTS AND HUNTERS HAD TO BELIEVE IN SOMETHING LIKE A COMMON WEALTH IN ORDER TO SHARE THEIR PROFITS WITH THE NEW PRIESTS, ARTISTS AND SOLDIERS.

BUT SOON A PROBLEM EMERGED: FREE RIDERS. SOME MEMBERS OF THE COMMUNITY DISCOVERED THAT THEY COULD BENEFIT FROM THE COMMON WEALTH AND, AT THE SAME TIME, FOSTER THEIR PERSONAL RICHNESS SIMPLY BY ELUDING THEIR CONTRIBUTIONS TO THE COMMUNITY AND HOLDING BACK CORN AND PREY. ESPECIALLY IN TIMES OF FAMINES OR WARS, THIS STRATEGY GAVE THEM AN EVOLUTIONARY ADVANTAGE OVER THOSE WHO CONTINUED TO COOPERATE.

UNFORTUNATELY, THIS MADE THE STRATEGY OF NOT COOPERATING AND NOT SHARING ALSO A RATIONAL SURVIVAL STRATEGY FROM DAY ONE.

ACCUMULATION OR COOPERATION? ~

IT'S OBVIOUS THAT THE FIRST HUMAN SOCIETIES HAD TO CONCORD ON RULES TO KEEP THESE EQUALLY REWARDING STRATEGIES IN THE BALANCE FOR THE GOOD OF ALL. FROM DAY ONE, POLITICS MEANT THE PROCESS OF COUNTERBALANCING COOPERATION AND ACCUMULATION IN ORDER TO ASSURE DECENT LIVING CONDITIONS FOR THE HIGHEST NUMBER OF COMMUNITY MEMBERS POSSIBLE.

BUT WHO HAD THE POWER TO DO SO? WHO WAS POWERFUL ENOUGH TO DECIDE WHAT EXACTLY EVERY SINGLE MEMBER OF THE COMMUNITY HAD TO CONTRIBUTE TO THE

COMMON WEALTH, AND HOW EXACTLY THE SURPLUS THAT THE COMMUNITY CREATED WAS DIVIDED AMONG THEIR MEMBERS?

IF YOU ARE LOOKING FOR THE "BIG BANG" OF INEQUALITY, YOU MIGHT FIND IT HERE: AN EVENING IN SPRING WHEN THE HUNTERS AND GATHERERS CAME TOGETHER TO ELECT ONE OF THEM TO BE "THE KEEPER"—THE WISE PERSON, HOLDER OF THE REGISTER, WHO WOULD FROM NOW ON DECIDE AT THE END OF EACH SUMMER WHO HAD TO GIVE AND WHO HAD TO RECEIVE WHAT.

BECAUSE, YOU SEE, ELECTING "THE KEEPER"—THAT IS, ESTABLISHING THE ROLE OF A TRIBE LEADER, A PREMIER, A MAJOR OR WHATEVER YOU WANT TO CALL IT—BORE A TERRIBLE RISK: WHAT IF THIS MAN, ONCE RAISED TO POWER BY POPULAR VOTE, WOULD USE THIS VERY POWER AGAINST THE POPULATION?

"THE KEEPER" BECOMES "THE KING" ~

AT A TIME WHEN A LIFESPAN WAS SHORT AND THE COLLECTIVE MEMORY ALMOST EXCLUSIVELY BASED ON STORIES, AN ELECTED "KEEPER" WITH LIMITED DECISIONAL POWER COULD BECOME A "GODSEND KING" IN A FEW YEARS AND HAND DOWN HIS OFFICE TO HIS NEXT OF KIN. AND THAT'S EXACTLY WHAT HAPPENED.

BY DECLARING THE DISTRIBUTION OF THE SURPLUS HIS GOD-GIVEN PRIVILEGE, THE "KEEPER" WAS NOW ABLE TO ACT WITHOUT CONSIDERATION OF THE COMMON GOOD. HE COULD MAINTAIN A PRIVATE ARMY OF LIFE GUARDS, IMPOSE LAWS AND, THROUGH THE SELLING OF COMMUNITY-LAND AND TRADE-RIGHTS, ENRICH HIMSELF AND HIS FAMILY.

BUT IN ORDER TO JUSTIFY HIS ACTIONS IN THE LONG RUN, EVEN THE MOST RUTHLESS RULER HAD TO CREATE AN IDEOLOGY, A STORY. "THE KEEPER", NOW A SELF-PROCLAIMED KING BY THE GRACE OF GOD, THUS HAD TO BECOME THE FIRST MARKETING- AND PRESENTATION-EXPERT IN HISTORY.

BY USING MONEY OR THREATS IN ORDER TO BEND POETS, BARDS AND PRIESTS TO HIS WILL, HE LEARNED NOT JUST TO CONTROL THE DAILY LIFE OF HIS SUBJECTS, BUT TO MANIPULATE ALSO THE LEGENDS AND STORIES OF HIS TRIBE— AND THEREFORE THE IDEAS OF HIS FORMER FELLOW CITIZENS.

THE NEW KINGS CONQUER THE WORLD ~

THIS IS THE FASCINATING AS WELL AS TRAGIC MOMENT IN HUMAN HISTORY WHEN THE FIRST VILLAGES WERE TRANSFORMED INTO CITIES WITH A RULER'S PALACE, A GOLDEN PALACE THAT LOOKED DOWN ON THE EVER-GROWING LOWER QUARTERS OF MISERY. THIS IS THE MOMENT WHEN THE DOMINION OF THE FEW OVER THE MANY BECAME NATURAL AND A COMMUNITY BASED ON EQUALITY ALMOST IMPOSSIBLE TO IMAGINE.

EVEN WORSE, AS SOON AS THE AUTHORITY OVER THEIR OWN COMMUNITY WAS MILITARILY, ECONOMICALLY AND CULTURALLY SECURED, THE FIRST SELF-PROCLAIMED KINGS TOOK A FOR THE HISTORY OF MANKIND FAR-REACHING NEXT STEP: THEY USED THE SURPLUS OF THEIR COMMUNITY TO CONQUER OTHER CENTRES OF POWER NEARBY.

A FATAL CLOCKWORK OF DICTATORSHIP ON THE INSIDE AND WARS OF CONQUEST ON THE OUTSIDE BEGAN TO UNFOLD. WITHIN THE NEXT THREE THOUSAND YEARS THE POWERFUL FEW WOULD CREATE MYTHS AND STORIES IN ORDER TO KEEP THEIR FELLOW CITIZENS IN POVERTY AND AT THE SAME TIME MAKE THEM PRODUCE MORE AND MORE SURPLUS, "FOR THE SAKE OF THE GREATNESS OF OUR NATION". WHY? BECAUSE THE FEW NEEDED MORE AND MORE MONEY TO BUILD MORE AND MORE SHIPS AND EXPEDITION CORPS TO FIGHT AND CONQUER MORE AND MORE OTHER KINGDOMS.

THE AGE OF THE GLOBAL WARS FOR LAND AND RESOURCES HAD BEGUN, THE AGE OF THE EXTERMINATION OF THE INCAS, MAYAS AND INDIANS IN THE AMERICAS IN ORDER TO STEAL THEIR GOLD AND THEIR LAND, THE AGE OF CHILD LABOUR AND FORCED INDUSTRIALISATION IN ENGLAND FOR THE SAKE OF THE BRITISH NAVY, THE AGE OF TOTAL PROPAGANDA AND TERROR IN JAPAN, ITALY AND GERMANY FOR THE SAKE OF THEIR CRAZY QUEST FOR FOREIGN POSSESSIONS.

IN THIS GLOBAL RACE, EVERY PARTICIPANT HAD THE SAME GOAL: TO SQUEEZE THE OWN NATIONAL POPULATION IN ORDER TO ACCUMULATE THE MEANS OF INTERNATIONAL DOMINATION FASTER THAN THE OTHER NATIONS.

THAT WAS—AND STILL IS—THE LAW OF GLOBAL CAPITALISM: "YOU HAVE TO ACCUMULATE FASTER THAN THE OTHERS AND BEAT THEM WITH EVERY MEAN AT YOUR DISPOSAL —BEFORE THEY CAN DO THE SAME TO YOU."

WILL YOU CHOOSE HOPE OR CYNICISM? ~

BUT EVEN DURING THOSE DARK AGES OF TERROR AND WARS, COOPERATION BETWEEN PEOPLE AND NATIONS NEVER CEASED COMPLETELY. THE FEW IN POWER COULD NOT PERMANENTLY WIPE OUT OUR HUMANITY AND OUR LONGING FOR CONNECTION AND LOVE. SOME OF US CONTINUED TO BELIEVE THAT THIS WORLD SHOULD BE A BEAUTIFUL PLACE FOR THE MANY AND NOT JUST FOR THE FEW.

TODAY, THIS STRUGGLE FOR THE FUTURE OF MANKIND IS BY NO MEANS OVER, NO, IT CONTINUES TO RAGE. THE FEW ARE STILL IN POWER, AND THE BATTLE BETWEEN A CYNICAL WORLD VIEW BASED ON PROFIT FOR SOME THROUGH THE EXPLOITATION OF ALL ON THE ONE HAND AND THE HEROIC ATTEMPT TO ESTABLISH A TRUE DEMOCRACY ON THE OTHER IS STILL RAGING ON.

THIS BATTLE IS THE MOST IMPORTANT BATTLE IN THE HISTORY OF MANKIND, AND YOU SHOULD ASK YOURSELF WHETHER YOU WANT TO REMAIN AMONG THOSE WHO PUT PROFIT ABOVE EVERYTHING ELSE, OR WHETHER YOU WANT TO FIGHT WITH US FOR A DEEP, PASSIONATE LIFE DEDICATED TO BROTHERHOOD AND JUSTICE—AND YOU SHOULD COMMUNICATE YOUR DECISION OPENLY IN YOUR PRESENTATIONS.

SO, TELL ME, TELL US, WHICH SIDE WILL YOU CHOOSE?

TIP ~

AS HUMAN BEINGS WE HAVE BEEN PROGRAMMED FOR MILLENNIA TO:

~ READ HUMAN FACES TO GUESS INTENTIONS (FRIEND OR FOE? ESCAPE OR FIGHT?).

THEREFORE, SMILE A LOT BECAUSE THANKS TO OUR MIRROR NEURONES, FEELINGS THAT WE PERCEIVE ON THE FACES OF OTHERS ARE TRIGGERED IN OURSELVES. HOWEVER, THIS ONLY APPLIES TO AUTHENTIC FEELINGS. NEVER LIE, FOR YOUR FACE WILL BETRAY YOU AS SOON AS YOU ARE NOT TELLING THE TRUTH.

~ PAY ATTENTION TO PEOPLE WHO BEHAVE IN AN UNUSUAL WAY (RIGHT OR WRONG? JOIN IN OR FIGHT IT?).

THAT'S WHY IT'S SO IMPORTANT TO OFFER YOUR AUDIENCE SOMETHING UNEXPECTED THAT ATTRACTS ATTENTION RIGHT FROM THE START: CHALLENGING IDEAS, EXTRAORDINARY STORIES & SURPRISING PHOTOGRAPHS.

~ TAKE NOTICE WHEN VALUES SUCH AS FAIRNESS & EQUALITY ARE QUESTIONED (ONLY IN HIS/ HER INTEREST OR IN MINE TOO? FAIR OR UNFAIR?).

NEVER TRY TO BRIBE YOUR AUDIENCE OR APPEAL TO THEIR SELFISHNESS. WE HUMANS WILL NEVER FOLLOW FRAUDSTERS & HATE-PREACHERS FOR LONG BECAUSE WE ALL WANT TO BE GOOD PEOPLE.

"THERE ARE NO PASSENGERS ON SPACESHIP EARTH. WE ARE ALL CREW."

~ MARSHALL MCLUHAN

WHAT DO YOU THINK AFTER HAVING READ THE SHORT CLIPPING ABOUT OUR PAST? APPARENTLY, A LOT WENT WRONG, RIGHT? AND YET IT SEEMS TO ME THAT OUR PRESENT DAYS SHINE IN A MUCH BRIGHTER LIGHT THAN ANY OTHER EPOCH BEFORE.

THE BEAUTIFUL BATTLEFIELD FOR THE FUTURE ~

IN FACT, TODAY YOUNG MEN AND WOMEN ALL OVER THE WORLD ARE CONNECTING VIA THE INTERNET AND DEMANDING THEIR FAIR SHARE OF PROSPERITY AND A MORE SUSTAINABLE AND HUMANE FUTURE FOR ALL OF US.

FROM THE MIGHTY SKYSCRAPERS OF WALL STREET TO THE GREEN PARKS OF ISTANBUL, FROM THE NARROW STREETS OF BURMA TO THE SHINING BUSINESS DISTRICTS OF PARIS, FROM THE STONE TOWERS OF SAN GIMIGNANO TO THE GREAT BARRIER REEF IN CAIRNS, AUSTRALIA, OUR WORLD HAS BECOME A BEAUTIFUL BATTLEFIELD FOR THE FUTURE.

FOLLOWING THE CALL OF FATE, MILLIONS OF MEN AND WOMEN LIKE ME AND YOU DEMAND CLEAN, AFFORDABLE ENERGY, COMPREHENSIVE EDUCATION AND MEANINGFUL JOBS FOR ALL. DO THEY DEMAND THE IMPOSSIBLE?

YES, IF "MORE, BIGGER AND FASTER" REMAINS THE BASIC PRINCIPLE OF OUR ECONOMY, YES, IF THE WEALTHY NATIONS CONTINUE TO REFUSE TO SHARE THEIR PROSPERITY WITH THE POOR OF THIS WORLD, YES, IF THE SHORT-SIGHTED EGOISM OF THE FEW CONTINUES TO BE PLACED ABOVE THE LEGITIMATE INTERESTS OF THE MANY.

A NEW ERA IS DAWNING ~

BUT THERE IS HOPE BECAUSE MORE AND MORE OF US REALISE THAT IN A FINITE WORLD THE BASIC ASSUMPTION OF CAPITALISM—ENDLESS GROWTH—IS NOT ONLY UNTRUE BUT INSANE. WE ARE ALREADY PRODUCING AND BUILDING,

EXTRACTING AND DESTROYING, CONSUMING AND DISPOSING OF MUCH MORE THAN OUR GLOBAL ECOSYSTEM COULD POSSIBLY WITHSTAND.

NO, WE ALL HAVE TO FACE THE FACT THAT WE CANNOT OVERCOME THE TERRIBLE UNEQUAL DISTRIBUTION OF WEALTH AND OPPORTUNITIES BY MAKING THE CAKE BIGGER AND BIGGER. WE HAVE TO REDISTRIBUTE THE CAKE. THIS WILL INITIALLY MAKE A FEW OF US POORER, YES, BUT IT WILL ALSO MAKE MILLIONS OF PEOPLE AROUND THE WORLD RICHER IN A SUSTAINABLE AND INSPIRING WAY.

AND WE HAVE ALSO OTHER MEANS TO INCREASE WEALTH ON A PLANETARY SCALE: THE CREATION OF A GLOBAL PRODUCTION- AND RECYCLING-CYCLE WILL LEAD TO ENORMOUS SAVINGS—MONEY THAT WE CAN INVEST IN EDUCATION AND RESEARCH IN THE YEARS TO COME. THE GLOBAL TAXATION OF FINANCIAL TRANSACTIONS AND PERSONAL WEALTH WILL HELP US TO FINANCE NEW, BETTER JOBS. AND IF WE INCREASE THE EXPORT OF OUR GREEN TECHNOLOGIES INSTEAD OF OUR ARMS SALES, WE CAN END GLOBAL WARMING, RESOURCE WARS AND UNCONTROLLED MIGRATION ALL OVER THE WORLD.

THIS IS OUR TIME! ~

I BELIEVE THAT OUR PRESENTATIONS ARE AN IMPORTANT MEANS OF MAKING PEOPLE UNDERSTAND THAT OUR FEW CITIES OF GOLD WILL COLLAPSE TOGETHER WITH THE SLUMS OF POVERTY IF WE DO NOT FINALLY BEGIN TO SHARE MORE JUSTLY —INSTEAD OF EXPLOITING OUR WORLD AND THE PEOPLE LIVING IN IT EVER FASTER AND MORE RADICALLY.

LET ME CONCLUDE THESE REMARKS ABOUT THE WORLD FROM WHICH WE ALL COME WITH A GLIMMER OF HOPE: AS FRIGHTENING AS THE CHALLENGES AHEAD MAY BE, THEY ARE ALSO BEAUTIFUL AND THRILLING. BEING PART OF A POWERFUL WAVE THAT WILL CHANGE THE COURSE OF OUR HISTORY IS A PRIVILEGE GRANTED TO ONLY A FEW GENERATIONS.

I HAVE ALL MY LIFE BEEN SURE OF ONE THING: THE MOMENT WE REKINDLE THE ETERNAL FLAME OF COURAGE IN OUR HEART, WE CAN ALL BECOME HEROES, REAL PEOPLE THAT OUR CHILDREN'S CHILDREN WILL REMEMBER WITH A SMILE ON THEIR FACES.

THIS IS OUR TIME, MY FRIEND!

TIP ~

LET'S GO BACK TO 10 JUNE 1963 AND START ANEW:

IT WAS ONE OF THOSE MOMENTS THAT CHANGE THE COURSE OF HISTORY: ON 19 OCTOBER 1962 US-PRESIDENT JOHN F. KENNEDY LISTENED TO HIS GENERALS' OPINION ON HOW TO SOLVE THE CUBAN MISSILE CRISIS. THEY ADVISED HIM TO DESTROY THE SOVIET BASES THROUGH AIR STRIKES, INVADE THE ISLAND & DEPOSE THE CUBAN LEADER FIDEL CASTRO.

BUT JACK KENNEDY HAD READ BARBARA TUCHMAN'S BOOK "THE GUNS OF AUGUST", IN WHICH THE MISJUDGMENTS OF THE MOST SENIOR MILITARY WERE BLAMED FOR THE OUTBREAK OF WORLD WAR I, & HE WAS APPALLED WHEN HE REALISED THAT HIS GENERALS CONSIDERED A POSSIBLE NUCLEAR WAR WITH THE SOVIET UNION A VIABLE STRATEGY.

THEREFORE, JFK DECIDED AGAINST HIS GENERALS, FAVOURING A SEA BLOCKADE OF CUBA INSTEAD, & DAYS LATER A SECRET AGREEMENT BETWEEN WASHINGTON AND MOSCOW— THE US PROMISED TO WITHDRAW ITS NUCLEAR MISSILES FROM TURKEY—LED TO THE DISMANTLING OF ALL SOVIET MISSILES ON CUBAN SOIL.

JFK HAD NEVER PLANNED TO QUESTION THE POWER OF THE "MILITARY-INDUSTRIAL COMPLEX", BUT THE CUBAN MISSILE CRISIS ON THE ONE HAND & THE CIVIL RIGHTS MOVEMENT LED BY MARTIN LUTHER KING ON THE OTHER CHANGED THE YOUNG PRESIDENT'S WORLD VIEW. HE BEGAN TO UNDERSTAND THAT ONLY SOCIAL JUSTICE IN HIS OWN COUNTRY & DIALOGUE WITH THE SOVIET UNION ON THE INTERNATIONAL STAGE COULD LEAD TO GENUINE FREEDOM & PEACE FOR ALL.

HOW MUCH JFK HAD CHANGED, BECAME CLEAR IN JUNE 1963 WHEN HE SPOKE AT THE COMMENCEMENT CEREMONY OF THE AMERICAN UNIVERSITY IN WASHINGTON. THIS SPEECH ON THE NECESSITY TO OVERCOME THE COLD WAR & TO BEGIN GLOBAL DISARMAMENT TALKS MEANT A DEPARTURE FROM THE LOGIC OF GLOBAL IMPERIALISM, THEREFORE DIRECTLY ENDANGERING THE PROFITS OF THE ARMAMENT- AND OIL-INDUSTRIES. I THINK THAT JFK FELL VICTIM TO A CONSPIRACY FIVE MONTHS LATER MAINLY BECAUSE OF THIS SPEECH.

"What kind of peace do I mean? What kind of peace do we seek? Not a Pax Americana enforced on the world by American weapons of war. Not the peace of the grave or the security of the slave. I am talking about genuine peace, the kind of peace that makes life on earth worth living, the kind that enables man and nations to grow and to hope and to build a better life for their children, not merely peace for Americans but for all men and women, not merely peace for our time but peace for all time.

I speak of peace because of the new face of war. Total war makes no sense in an age when great powers can maintain large and relatively invulnerable nuclear forces and refuse to surrender without resorting to those forces. It makes no sense in an age when a single nuclear weapon contains almost ten times the explosive force delivered by all of Allied Air Forces in the Second World War. It makes no sense in an age when the deadly poisons produced by a nuclear exchange would be carried by the wind and water and soil and seed to the far corners of the globe and to generations unborn.

I speak of peace, therefore, as the necessary rational end of rational men. I realise that the pursuit of peace is not as dramatic as the pursuit of war, and frequently the words of the pursuer of peace fall on deaf ears. But we have no more urgent task."

The crossfire in Dallas on 22 November 1963 was nothing less than a coup, triggering the chain of events that would lead many years later to the election of George W. Bush & the US-wars in the Middle East. As a result, we have lost fifty years of possible social progress for the Many & instead have to endure governments that divert our hard-earned wealth into the death-smelling pockets of a few shareholders in the so-called defence industry & oil-companies.

The speech against Imperialism & war & its profiteers delivered by John Fitzgerald Kennedy on 10 June 1963 is the point from which we all must start anew today.

"FEW PEOPLE WILL HAVE THE GREATNESS TO BEND HISTORY ITSELF; BUT EACH OF US CAN WORK TO CHANGE A SMALL PORTION OF EVENTS, AND IN THE TOTAL OF ALL THOSE ACTS WILL BE WRITTEN THE HISTORY OF THIS GENERATION."

~ ROBERT F. KENNEDY

So far, I have tried to show you that our generation is facing the most difficult task in human history, but also has an historic opportunity to make this world a better place for all of us tomorrow.

To be successful, all of our presentations should address one or more of these ten problems:

- Short-term oriented capitalism.
- The uncontrolled power of big corporations.
- The uncontrolled power of oligarchs.
- The uncontrolled power of secret organisations.
- Global inequality.
- Totalitarian surveillance by state agencies.
- Human rights negation and violation.
- Toxic production cycles and Energy management.
- Global warming and climate disruptions.
- Fading biodiversity.
- A global arms race.

There is no private happiness ~

If you really want to change the world, you have to think and act local, national and international: through political actions on the ground, through your decisions as a consumer and through your work as a teacher, student, worker, scientist, politician, artist, doctor, service provider, manager or CEO.

You and I are both citizens of the world, and as such we must act, for there will be no "little happiness" left when tsunamis and tornadoes will have devastated our cities, and social unrest and wars will have destroyed the lives of those we love. We must realise that none of us can be happy and successful in

A WORLD THAT FAILS, AS JØRGEN RANDERS PUTS IT SO APTLY IN HIS BOOK "2052".

THAT IS WHY OUR PRESENTATIONS MUST ALSO SPEAK FOR THOSE WHO DO NOT YET HAVE A VOICE. THE STREET CHILDREN IN RIO DE JANEIRO OR MUMBAI DO NOT HAVE THE CHANCE TO GIVE LECTURES, AND THE AMAZON DOLPHIN, THE SIBERIAN TIGER OR THE VALUABLE TREES OF THE SINHARAJA RAINFOREST DO NOT HAVE THIS POSSIBILITY EITHER.

IT IS THEREFORE OUR TASK TO FIND AND PRESENT SOLUTIONS THAT WORK EQUALLY FOR ALL PLANTS, ANIMALS AND PEOPLE ON EARTH AS WELL AS FOR US.

BE INCLUSIVE, NOT EXCLUSIVE ~

CONSEQUENTLY, OUR PRESENTATIONS MUST BE AS INCLUSIVE AS POSSIBLE, THEY MUST BE MANIFESTOS FOR A WORLD IN WHICH NO ONE IS EXPLOITED, NO FUNDAMENTAL RIGHTS ARE DENIED AND EVERYONE FINALLY BENEFITS FROM THE MANY BLESSINGS OF PROGRESS.

THIS IS NOT NAIVE ALTRUISM, BUT TRUE REALISM IF WE WANT TO SAVE OURSELVES AND THE PEOPLE WE LOVE. AT SOME POINT OF OUR LIVES, WE WILL BE "THE OTHERS", AT SOME POINT, WE WILL BE THE FORGOTTEN, DISENFRANCHISED AND PERSECUTED, HOWEVER GOOD WE ARE AT THE MOMENT, AND THAT IS ONE MORE GOOD REASON WHY OUR PRESENTATIONS SHOULD ALWAYS BE ABOUT GIVING OUR VOICE TO THE FORGOTTEN, DISENFRANCHISED AND PERSECUTED.

OUR PRESENTATIONS ARE INSPIRING WHENEVER THEY DESIGN A VISION FOR A COMMON FUTURE. IN AN ERA OF ECONOMIC MONOPOLIES, DIGITAL TRIBES AND SPECIAL INTERESTS, OFFERS TO ACT TOGETHER ARE RARE BUT MORE NECESSARY THAN EVER.

DEEP IN OUR HEARTS WE KNOW THAT EACH OF US IS CONNECTED TO EVERY OTHER LIVING BEING, AND THAT NOTHING CAN BE CHANGED, EXPLOITED AND DESTROYED WITHOUT AFFECTING ALSO OURSELVES. DEEP IN OUR HEARTS WE KNOW THAT NOTHING CAN REALLY BE POSSESSED BECAUSE EVERYTHING BELONGS TO US ALL EQUALLY. DEEP IN OUR HEARTS WE KNOW THAT NOTHING WE CAN BUY CAN REALLY SATISFY US BECAUSE TRUE SATISFACTION ARISES FROM US BECOMING MORE AND MORE CONNECTED.

TRY THE CODESHARING PROGRAM (CSP):

IN YOUR PRESENTATIONS, MEETINGS & DISCUSSIONS YOU SHOULD ADDRESS & ANSWER FOUR TYPES OF "COLOUR QUESTIONS":

~ YELLOW: "IS OUR PRODUCT OR SERVICE DESIGNED TO MAKE THE WORLD A BETTER PLACE? HOW EXACTLY?"

~ GREEN: "DOES OUR PRODUCT OR SERVICE HELP OUR CUSTOMERS TO CHANGE & GROW FOR THE BETTER? HOW EXACTLY?"

~ RED: "WHAT POSSIBLE SIDE EFFECTS DOES OUR PRODUCT OR SERVICE HAVE FOR OUR CUSTOMERS, FAMILIES, FRIENDS & THE ENVIRONMENT?"

~ BLUE: "WOULD WE WANT OUR FAMILY & FRIENDS TO USE OUR PRODUCT OR SERVICE, WOULD WE WANT TO LIVE IN A WORLD WHERE EVERYONE USES IT?"

BY ADDING A THIN YELLOW, GREEN, RED OR BLUE LINE ON YOUR SLIDES, FLYERS OR E-MAILS, YOU CAN SHOW YOUR AUDIENCE THAT YOUR CURRENT TEXT, CHART OR PIECE OF DATA REFERS TO THAT PARTICULAR QUESTION.

"TREE PLANTING IS ALWAYS A UTOPIAN ENTERPRISE, IT SEEMS TO ME, A WAGER ON A FUTURE THE PLANTER DOESN'T NECESSARILY EXPECT TO WITNESS."

~ MICHAEL POLLAN

As part of humanity, today each of us is living between the pure light of the stars above our heads and the mud of the endless suburbs, factories and dumps at our feet. Over the time span of a thousand generations, our spirituality, our arts and the better part of our sciences have shown us the way to the stars, while we have at the same time repeatedly lost ourselves in inequality, exploitation and war here on earth:

~ Although we have gained a new feeling for the beauty of nature that our ancestors, being a part of it, could not have, we have at the same time destroyed much of the realm of our Mother Earth in the process.

~ Although we have expanded our knowledge of our universe, we have at the same time killed the wise and loving mermaids, fairies and sorcerers who inhabited the oceans, forests and mountains of our ancestors.

~ Although we have gained personal freedom of choice, we have at the same time lost the reassuring sense of community and belonging that our ancestors still possessed.

THE TREE OF LIFE ~

This brokenness, from which we all come and that we do carry with us where ever we go, is reflected in everything we do: we are broken beings, and, accordingly, nothing in our society is really accomplished and absolutely good. Our Tree of Life is sick, and we must try the almost impossible and heal its roots, the trunk and the branches while we continue to grow and reach for the stars and distant horizons.

Before we go on stage to present, we should, therefore, ask ourselves how we can contribute to the healing of our audience and the world as a whole:

- ~ How can I satisfy my listeners' need to feel safe and respected? (roots)

- ~ How can I help my listeners to feel loved and part of a community? (trunk)

- ~ How can I help my audience to gain more self-confidence and courageously realise their dreams? (branches and leaves)

- ~ How can I meet and foster my audience's need for personal growth and self-realisation? (crown)

If you make sure that your presentation meets these four basic human needs of each of your listeners, it can become a healing and inspiring moment for all of them.

Utopia is calling you ~

Healing enables growth by uniting the opposites of our history on a higher level, thus liberating our true potential as humanity for the first time. "But", you might ask, "healing for what, potential for what, to gain which horizons?"

You will find the answer to this questions in the thousands of stories, legends and myths of our ancestors which, however different they may seem to us at first glance, all revolve around the same hidden knowledge: that there is another, seemingly impossible and distant world—Utopia—which is reaching out for us and which will fulfil our needs far more than this one.

I say "reaching out for us" because this wonderful world, in which we will finally live together as real people, seems to talk to us from our future and influence everything we do in our present. Or how else can it be explained that every poem, every book, every statue, every prayer, every great speech and every great presentation that has ever come into being referred to Utopia in one way or another?

But be warned, my friend, Utopia waiting there for us in our future does not mean that this bright future will come into existence all by itself. Utopia needs us in order to become reality because the vision of a truly humane future is in constant danger of being made invisible by a "logic" that reduces the meaning of life to the production and purchase of chocolate bars, washing powder and cars.

Mentors like Albert Einstein, Mahatma Gandhi, John and Robert Kennedy, Nelson Mandela and many others have repeatedly tried to make us see that and lead us back onto the path for Utopia. And now, in the era of the Internet, their inspiring speeches, together with a billion other authentic, uncensored and revolutionary ideas, show us what we must do.

In order to become real people and finally make Utopia our home, we will all have to stand together against the Few and their dark logic. What awaits us, are total surveillance, soldiers on the streets and wars waged on our behalf, "against human rights violations, terrorism and dictatorships", but in reality waged against true democracy and true humanity and therefore against ourselves, the Many.

Believe me, all these dangers are real, and I am aware of the fact that it will take all our courage to confront them. Nevertheless, face them we must, there is no alternative. We are destined for another, better world, but real prosperity, real justice and real democracy will not come about on their own.

Let me say it once again: the future needs us, you and me, to become reality for us.

How long are you going to pretend you don't hear the call of Utopia?

Chapter one ~
The waves of our soul

"THE FIRST STEP TO THE KNOWLEDGE OF THE WONDER AND MYSTERY OF LIFE IS ... THE REALISATION THAT THIS IS JUST AS IT IS AND THAT IT CANNOT AND WILL NOT BE CHANGED. THOSE WHO THINK THEY KNOW HOW THE UNIVERSE COULD HAVE BEEN HAD THEY CREATED IT—WITHOUT PAIN, WITHOUT SORROW, WITHOUT TIME, WITHOUT DEATH—ARE UNFIT FOR ILLUMINATION."

~ JOSEPH CAMPBELL

YOU NEVER DID NOT EXIST, YOU ARE IMMORTAL, BUT AT SOME POINT YOU DECIDED TO BE BORN AS A HUMAN BEING. THIS IS OUR COMMON DESTINY: IN ORDER TO BE ABLE TO FEEL, DEVELOP AND SHARE THE WISDOM, COMPASSION AND LOVE WITHIN US, WE HAD TO ACQUIRE A BODY. AS A RESULT WE CAN AND MUST LIVE IN A PHYSICAL WORLD WITH ALL ITS OPPOSITES, THAT IS, WITH ALL THE HAPPINESS AND WITH ALL THE SUFFERING THAT ARE POSSIBLE WITHIN IT.

THE GAME OF LIFE ~

BIRTH AND DEATH, DAY AND NIGHT, YOUTH AND OLD AGE, CALM AND UNREST, LOVE AND FEAR, PEACE AND WAR, HARMONY AND DESTRUCTION: LIFE. THIS IS WHAT WE WANTED. WE HAVE STEPPED OUT OF THE STATE OF UNCONSCIOUS PERFECTION TO PLAY THE GAME OF LIFE, WE HAVE CHOSEN TO BECOME BROKEN, IMPERFECT AND STRUGGLING BEINGS IN SEARCH OF CONSCIOUSNESS AND LOVE. SO THE FIRST FUNDAMENTAL TRUTH ON THE SPIRITUAL LEVEL THAT WE NEED TO UNDERSTAND IS THIS:

~ THE WAVES PRODUCED BY THE OPPOSITES OF EXISTENCE CREATE A WORLD IN WHICH THERE MUST BE SUFFERING IN ORDER TO ALLOW US TO PROGRESS TOWARDS HAPPINESS AND LOVE.

YOU CAN'T STOP THE WAVES OF LIFE FROM BREAKING AGAINST YOU, YOU CAN ONLY CHOOSE TO FACE THEM COURAGEOUSLY AND LEARN TO PLAYFULLY RIDE THEM. TO LIVE AS A HUMAN BEING MEANS TO ACCEPT THE WAVES OF LIFE, TO

GROW WHILE SURFING THEM AND TO FINALLY TRANSCEND EVERY SINGLE WAVE INTO A MOMENT OF LOVE.

~ ANGER, BOREDOM, GRIEF, FINANCIAL WORRIES, HATRED AND ILLNESS: ALL THIS IS INEVITABLY—ALSO—PART OF OUR LIVES. FEELINGS COME AND GO, PEOPLE APPROACH US AND MOVE ON AGAIN AND THINGS SOMETIMES GO WRONG.

YOU CAME INTO THE WORLD TO EXPERIENCE HAPPINESS AND SUFFERING, SO LEARN TO SURF THE WAVES AND TO LIVE A FULL, BEAUTIFUL AND DIFFICULT LIFE.

DON'T LIMIT YOUR LIFE BY TRYING TO AVOID DIFFICULT EXPERIENCES. YOUR LIFE WILL NOT BECOME CAREFREE THAT WAY, ON THE CONTRARY, YOU WILL FIRST LOSE YOUR ENERGY AND THEN THE JOY OF LIFE ITSELF.

~ THERE'S MORE THAN ONE WAY TO RIDE THE WAVES.

LIVE A UNIQUE LIFE, YOUR UNIQUE AND UNREPEATABLE LIFE, OR AS ANDY IRONS SO BEAUTIFULLY PUTS IT, "THERE ARE A MILLION WAYS TO RIDE THE WAVES, AND AS LONG AS YOU SMILE YOU DO IT RIGHT." DON'T TRY TO BE ANYBODY ELSE. YOU ENTERED THIS LIFE TO BE AS UNIQUE AND MYSTERIOUS AS YOUR SMILE, AS YOUR VOICE, AS YOUR WAY OF SEEING THE WORLD—AND NOT IN ORDER TO BE PERFECT. YOU HAVE TO GROW, YES, AND YOU SHOULD NEVER HURT PEOPLE, YES, BUT OTHERWISE YOU ARE FREE. SPEAK IN YOUR OWN WAY, SING IN YOUR OWN WAY AND PRESENT WITH YOUR OWN STYLE.

~ THERE ARE ALL KINDS OF WAVES, AND YOU SHOULDN'T JUST BE LOOKING FOR THE BIG ONES.

SOME OF US PERFORM OUTSTANDING FEATS EARLY ON, WRITE BESTSELLERS, WIN SPORTS TITLES OR BUILD GLOBAL COMPANIES. DO YOU ENVY THESE PEOPLE? YOU SHOULDN'T, BECAUSE THE REAL GOAL OF YOUR EXISTENCE IS TO BECOME A LIVING AND LOVING BEING, AND TO ACHIEVE THIS YOU DON'T HAVE TO RIDE THE BIGGEST WAVES.

NONE OF US GET EVERYTHING HE OR SHE HAS HOPED FOR, BELIEVE ME, NOBODY DOES. BUT THAT DOESN'T MATTER. IT IS IMPORTANT THAT YOU TAKE EVERY WAVE, BOTH SMALL AND LARGE ONES, IN STYLE AND ALWAYS KEEP AN EYE ON YOUR GUIDING STAR HIGH ABOVE YOU. TO LIVE YOUR UNIQUE, UNMISTAKABLE AND UNREPEATABLE LIFE IS THE GREATEST HAPPINESS THERE IS IN THE UNIVERSE.

"That is part of the beauty of all literature. You discover that your longings are universal longings, that you are not lonely and isolated from anyone. You belong."

~ F. Scott Fitzgerald

Maybe you have already found a mentor in real life, a friend, a relative or a coach to help you, but maybe not. Then you should look not only at the present time, but at all times—and read. I myself loved literature as a child, and I think that the great writers I have met there over the years have saved my life.

Anton Pavlovich Chekhov ~

From the peak of my fifty-plus years, I can clearly see today that the discovery of classical Russian literature was one of the turning points in my life. Meeting Tolstoy, Turgenev, Gogol, Pushkin and especially Chekhov helped me to understand the nature of my soul and to more and more accept myself as a person.

I remember exactly how grateful I felt when I first read Anton Chekhov's stories and plays. His short story "Rothschild's Violin" is one of the most shocking works I have ever met in art, and his life and death—he died prematurely of tuberculosis at the age of 44—touched me deeply.

There was someone who was able to feel and describe every single thorn in a person's existence and who was still in love with life! That is why I loved Chekhov from the very first moment, him and his clear-sighted compassion, and why I am still loving him today. And that is why, although I've never met him in the physical world, he became one of my mentors.

ERNEST HEMINGWAY ~

Not far from a pontoon bridge sits an old man on the side of the road. Trucks and soldiers of the Spanish Republican Army cross the bridge, they are on the run, as are many civilians following them. But the old man is not moving. "I was taking care of animals", the old man will explain to the narrator over and over again. His heart is broken because he had to flee the city of San Carlos because of the artillery fire of the Fascists and leave the animals behind: two goats, a cat and four pairs of pigeons.

He sits there, as the bridge over the Ebro becomes a more dangerous place by the minute because the Fascist troops can no longer be far away, and all he can think about are the animals he had to abandon. Nothing comforting is left of the time before the war: no more certainties, no compassion for man and animal and no hope for the future. All there is now is war.

The dialogue between the narrator and the old man at the bridge lasts no longer than a few minutes, and the story about the Spanish Civil War ends before it really begins. Hemingway does not tell us if the old man finally got up to cross the bridge and save himself, and we will never know if the animals he had taken care of in San Carlos survived the attack on the city.

Nevertheless, this is one of the most important short stories ever written, and it is one of the most impressive human documents against the atrocities of war.

You know, I learned something very important from Hemingway, something that every author and everyone who wants to present should take to heart: the real message is not in what we write, say or present, the real message—our truth—will appear between our lines, sentences and slides.

The essential always remains unspoken, but maybe this is precisely why it resonates in the hearts and souls of our audience.

RAYMOND CHANDLER ~

There are three challenges you have to face as an author as well as someone who wants to present successfully: Your first sentence must immediately attract the attention of your audience, the hero of your story must be loved by the audience and the last sentence of your novel or presentation must leave a deep impression in the hearts and minds of your listeners or readers. Perhaps there is even a fourth challenge: you always have to create moments of humour, no matter how serious your subject is, because humour, even the black one, gives us all hope.

Raymond Chandler was a true genius at mastering all four challenges. He created beautiful first lines, wrote, together with Scott Fitzgerald, the most touching final lines, he makes you fall in love with his hero Philip Marlowe on page one and he always makes you laugh, even though he describes a world as cold and forsaken as a painting by Edward Hopper.

Chandler's private eye Philip Marlowe is not an intellectual, he is not a businessman, he is not a husband and father, and we never know if he really believes in anything like a divine justice. But we can feel on every page that Marlowe is a beautiful person: wise, courageous and loving.

Marlowe is all a man can be, and yet, in the Los Angeles of the 1930s and 1940s, he can't help but feeling alone and sometimes even lonely. But it's exactly this tender despair that makes Philip Marlowe deep and compassionate as he fights for a better world without using a lot of words.

WILLIAM SHAKESPEARE ~

Johann Wolfgang von Goethe admired Shakespeare for his "beautiful rarity box" which can show us the history of the whole world on a small wooden stage. Goethe understood precisely what makes Shakespeare's work so outstanding: "It is said that he portrayed the Romans excellently. I don't think so, they are all inveterate Englishmen, but, of course, they are real people, people from the ground up, and therefore a Roman toga suits them just as well".

THIS IS ONE OF THE CORNERSTONES ON WHICH BOTH THE ART OF WRITING AND THE ART OF PRESENTATION REST: THE ABILITY TO SHOW YOUR AUDIENCE THE ESSENTIAL TRAITS OF HUMAN NATURE BEHIND THE CHANGING MASKS OF CULTURE, HISTORY AND INDIVIDUAL NARCISSISM THAT WE ALL SHARE.

ONCE WE HAVE ACHIEVED THIS MASTERY AS SPEAKERS, OUR PRESENTATION, WHETHER IT TELLS A STORY FROM THE PAST, FROM THE PRESENT OR FROM A DISTANT FUTURE, WILL SOUND FAMILIAR TO EVERY SINGLE PERSON IN THE AUDIENCE AND TOUCH THEM.

AUTHORS ARE VALUABLE MENTORS FOR US ~

BY NOW, YOU PROBABLY REALISE WHY WRITERS CAN SERVE YOU AS VALUABLE MENTORS ON YOUR WAY TO MASTERY IN THE ART OF PRESENTATION. AS DIFFERENT AS THEIR STORIES AND HEROES MAY SEEM TO US, THEIR CONCERN OVER THE CENTURIES IS ALWAYS THE SAME: TO HELP US TO BECOME MORE CONSCIOUS AND TO WORK FOR A NEW WORLD THAT IS MORE HUMANE.

UNTIL ONE DAY WE WILL BE BRAVE ENOUGH TO TAKE THEIR PLACE AND INSPIRE OTHER PEOPLE TO DO THE SAME.

"Without music, life would be a mistake."

~ Friedrich Nietzsche

Have you ever wondered where our languages come from? Personally, I think that all our languages stem from music, and that our songs have gradually turned into poems and stories.

The magic of sounds ~

If that's true, the sounds you produce with your voice while delivering your presentation are probably as important as the words you choose to get your audience to listen. As small babies we all learned to recognise the intention behind our parents' words by their sound, long before we could understand their meaning, and the people in your audience do the same.

So, if the sound of your words does not match what you say—for example, if you speak about sad things with a joyful voice or about joyful things with a sad one—your audience will immediately become aware of this discrepancy and doubt your sincerity from the first moment of your presentation. Above all, your audience will not feel the joy that comes only with harmony, or better, in this case, with harmonies.

The magic of anticipation ~

The second important characteristic that our language has inherited from music is the magical effect of anticipation. Music, even sad music, makes us so happy because it appeals directly to the reward system in our brain. A certain combination of notes allows us to predict in a fraction of a second which notes will follow, and if we are correct with our anticipation, and these notes actually resound, our brain releases happiness hormones as a reward.

Interestingly, a prediction that culminates in an even more perfect but unforeseen harmony, triggers even more well-being in us, and the same applies to

POEMS, STORIES AND PRESENTATIONS. THEY ALSO REWARD US BY GIVING US CLUES TO WHAT IS TO COME, BUILDING UP TENSION AND FINALLY CONDENSING THIS VERY TENSION INTO THE ALMOST ORGIASTIC EXPERIENCE OF A HARMONIOUS SOLUTION.

THAT'S WHY YOUR PRESENTATIONS NEED HINTS ON WHAT'S YET TO COME, RECURRENT HIGHLIGHTS AND A NARRATIVE STRUCTURE THAT CREATES EXCITEMENT AND ANTICIPATION FOR THE SOLUTION OF THE DISCUSSED PROBLEM: THIS WAY YOU CAN ENSURE THAT YOUR AUDIENCE WILL FEEL REWARDED AT THE END OF EACH SECTION OF YOUR PRESENTATIONS AND AFTER HAVING FOLLOWED IT STEP BY STEP TO THE END.

THE MAGIC OF THE FIRST LINE ~

THE THIRD MAGICAL QUALITY THAT OUR LANGUAGE HAS INHERITED FROM MUSIC IS ITS ABILITY TO DESCRIBE OUR ATTITUDE TOWARDS LIFE IN A FEW WORDS. LOOK AT THESE LINES OF THREE FAMOUS SONGS:

"A LONG, LONG TIME AGO, I STILL CAN REMEMBER HOW THIS MUSIC USED TO MAKE ME SMILE" (AMERICAN PIE, DON MCLEAN).

"THERE'S A LADY WHO'S SURE ALL THAT GLITTERS IS GOLD, AND SHE'S BUYING A STAIRWAY TO HEAVEN" (STAIRWAY TO HEAVEN, LED ZEPPELIN).

"I SEE A RED DOOR, AND I WANT TO PAINT IT BLACK" (PAINT IT BLACK, THE ROLLING STONES).

NO MATTER HOW TECHNICAL OR ACADEMIC THE TOPIC OF YOUR PRESENTATION MAY SEEM TO YOU AT FIRST, IF YOU CREATE A BRIGHT FIRST LINE THAT SHOWS US HOW YOU SEE LIFE, THE PEOPLE IN THE ROOM WILL BE INTERESTED AT ONCE IN WHAT YOU HAVE TO OFFER THEM.

ALWAYS REMEMBER: TO PRESENT MEANS ALSO "TO MAKE MUSIC". SO, PRACTICE YOUR VOICE, MAKE IT AS FULL, AS SMOOTH AND AS MELODIOUS AS POSSIBLE. LEARN TO CREATE ANTICIPATION, TURN EXPECTED HIGHLIGHTS INTO EVEN MORE SATISFYING MOMENTS WITH SURPRISING TWISTS AND TURNS, AND START YOUR PRESENTATIONS WITH AN ARTISTIC FIRST LINE THAT IMMEDIATELY REVEALS YOUR VIEW OF THE WORLD.

**"Cinema is a matter of what's in the frame
and what's out."**

~ Martin Scorsese

One of the biggest challenges in the field of communication today is to be able to decide which content should be expressed through which medium and how. Every talented artist is aware of the uniqueness of his or her medium, but also of its limits.

For example, a song can evoke emotions much faster than a novel, but the development of a person's life over many years can be expressed much better through a novel.

A photograph is as visual as a painting, but both create a different temperature in the representation of people and things: photography is usually the colder medium.

The three-dimensionality of a sculpture creates a more immediate way of encounter than a painting or photograph, while the cuts in a film create a breathtaking effect that a painting, photograph or sculpture usually will not be able to evoke.

When it comes to the art of presentation, you should therefore ask yourself the following question: "How can I best use the strengths, but also the limits of this art form to effectively convey my message to my audience?"

In my opinion, the art of presentation is most comparable to the art of filmmaking. In fact, both use the classic narrative format of Joseph Campbell's "Hero's Journey" which describes the overcoming of resistance and crises, the slow transformation of the hero and the final battle between good and evil.

Moreover, in both art forms the narrator uses images to show us the world in his or her unique way, thus changing our view of things in a compelling and lasting manner.

WHAT CAN WE LEARN FROM CINEMA? ~

In a good film as in a good presentation, some of our assumptions about things, people and the world are questioned and permanently changed.

"A rich girl and a poor boy can't be happy together", "Love cannot conquer death", "Time makes even the most precious feelings fade away". The 1997-block buster "Titanic" questions all these assumptions about the essence of love. In James Cameron's masterpiece, the supposedly unsinkable ship becomes a symbol of a society so fascinated by its material achievements that it has forgotten the never—ending power of true love. Sitting in the cinema chair, we can suddenly see love in all its fascinating facets.

A good film opens up a new view on the world as a whole, interestingly, by limiting itself to the essential. A good presentation opens our soul, our mind and our heart to the possibilities that we weren't aware of before, it offers us a new meaning, it tells our heart, "So much more is possible!"

That's why a good presentation relates to a bad one the way a good film relates to a traffic camera. It's all about your ability to limit yourself to what you consider essential (focus), to put it into a new context (frame) and to interpret it differently than anyone has done before (interpretation).

HELP PEOPLE TO RISE HIGHER ~

Every art form is like a pair of wings that makes us rise higher as human beings as well as humanity. Therefore, you should sing, read poems and perhaps write your own, watch as many films as possible and consider painting or taking a sculpture course, maybe even in Pietrasanta in Tuscany, a place not far from where I am writing you these lines right now.

Presenting is an art, and in order to understand its unique potential, you should try as many other forms of artistic expression as possible. Search and find your own unmistakable way to express yourself, surprise us, shock us, move us to tears, but show us your way to a new world and better future.

TIP ~

BECOME A SPIRITUAL MENTOR FOR OTHERS:

~ Clear your feelings, learn to love yourself before you begin to shine for the benefit of others.

~ Take the time to listen & ask questions, but do not give advice. Listen actively, without judging.

~ Do not solve the problems of others, but encourage & strengthen them in their attempt to solve them on their own. Trust the universal knowledge that lies dormant in every human being.

~ Try to accompany people lovingly, but without any attachment. Be aware that in most cases you will only be a station on their path to awareness.

"DESPITE ALL THE CHARACTERISTICS THAT DIFFERENTIATE US—RACE, LANGUAGE, RELIGION, GENDER, WEALTH AND MANY OTHERS—WE ARE ALL EQUAL IN TERMS OF OUR BASIC HUMANITY."

~ THE DALAI LAMA

WE HUMANS CAN ONLY SURVIVE AND THRIVE IN AN ENVIRONMENT OF TENDERNESS, LOVE AND CARE. FROM OUR FIRST DAY ON THIS EARTH, WE ARE CONNECTED AS MEMBERS OF A GREAT HUMAN COMMUNITY, AND ALTHOUGH EACH OF US IS BORN INTO VERY DIFFERENT FAMILIES, NATIONS AND CULTURES, WE ALL ASPIRE TO THE SAME THINGS:

~ WE ALL TRY TO AVOID PHYSICAL AND MENTAL SUFFERING.

~ WE ALL TRY TO FIND HAPPINESS AND LOVE.

~ WE'RE ALL TRYING TO MAKE SENSE OF THE STORY OF OUR LIFE.

I BELIEVE THAT THIS IS THE BASIS OF OUR COMMON HUMANITY, AND THAT MEANS THAT IF WE EXPLOIT, HURT OR KILL OTHER LIVING BEINGS, WE COMMIT A CRIME AGAINST THIS HUMAN NATURE COMMON TO ALL OF US—AND THEREFORE ALSO AGAINST OURSELVES.

THE "GOLDEN RULE" ~

IN A WORLD WHERE THE BASIC PRINCIPLES OF HUMANITY ARE IGNORED, NONE OF US CAN REALLY BE HAPPY.

THAT'S WHY YOU HAVE TO TREAT THE OTHERS THE WAY YOU WANT TO BE TREATED. IT'S NO COINCIDENCE YOU FIND THIS "GOLDEN RULE" IN EVERY MORAL CODE IN OUR HISTORY.

BUT THERE IS A PROBLEM: WE LIVE ON A PLANET WHERE FOR CENTURIES THE "GOLDEN RULE" HAS BEEN SUPPRESSED FOR THE BENEFIT OF A FEW INDIVIDUALS, COMPANIES AND COUNTRIES.

THE RESULT IS A WORLD IN WHICH 0.7% OF THE WORLD'S POPULATION NOW OWNS 40% OF ALL WEALTH, WHILE 2 BILLION PEOPLE—OUR BROTHERS AND SISTERS—STILL LIVE IN EXTREME POVERTY.

OUR HUMANITY IS THE ESSENCE OF BEING HUMAN ~

I THINK YOU WILL AGREE WITH ME WHEN I SAY THAT WE MUST OVERCOME THE SHORT-SIGHTED AND ESSENTIALLY INHUMAN PROFIT-THINKING THAT PREVAILS TODAY AND REPLACE IT WITH THE "GOLDEN RULE" AGAIN.

"YOU CAN FOOL THE WHOLE WORLD DOWN THE PATHWAY OF YEARS, AND GET PATS ON THE BACK AS YOU PASS, BUT YOUR FINAL REWARD WILL BE HEARTACHES AND TEARS, IF YOU'VE CHEATED THE GUY IN THE GLASS."

~ DALE WIMBROW

THERE IS ONE TASK, THE MOST IMPORTANT AND AT THE SAME TIME MOST DIFFICULT THAT YOU MUST ACCOMPLISH IN YOUR LIFE: YOU MUST GROW, DEVELOP SELF-LOVE AND FINALLY HELP OTHERS TO DO THE SAME.

EVERY INJUSTICE, VIOLENCE AND MILITARY ACTION HAS ITS ROOTS IN A LACK OF GROWTH, SELF-LOVE AND LOVE. IF YOU CAN DEDICATE YOUR LIFE TO LOVE, WE WILL ALL FEEL MORE LOVE. IF YOU FAIL, IT WILL BE HARDER ON ALL OF US. YOU ARE THE UNIVERSE, YOU ARE THE WORLD, YOU ARE ALL OF US.

OUR WORLD NEEDS YOU ~

OUR UNIVERSE IS, AT LEAST IN MY VIEW, A HOLOGRAPHY THAT THINKS AND FEELS: THAT IS WHY EVERY LITTLE CHANGE IN YOUR INNER BEING CHANGES EVERYTHING AROUND YOU, AND VICE VERSA.

IN THIS SENSE, THERE IS NO "PERSONAL GROWTH", NO "PRIVATE HAPPINESS" AND NO "LIMITED LOVE".

THEREFORE, THE QUESTION REALLY IS: ARE YOU READY TO GROW AND AT THE SAME TIME HELP OTHERS TO GROW? ARE YOU GOOD TO YOURSELF AND AT THE SAME TIME HELPING OTHER PEOPLE TO BE GOOD TO THEMSELVES AND TO OTHERS? DO YOU TRY TO ACCEPT AND GIVE MORE LOVE AND AT THE SAME TIME HELP OTHERS TO DO THE SAME?

YOUR HABITS MAKE A HUGE DIFFERENCE ~

IF YOUR ANSWER TO ONE OR MORE OF THESE QUESTIONS IS "NO", YOU HAVE TO CHANGE YOUR HABITS BECAUSE YOUR HABITS DETERMINE YOUR LIFE:

~ WHICH OF YOUR HABITS ARE GOOD FOR YOUR SPIRITUAL, MENTAL, EMOTIONAL AND PHYSICAL GROWTH, AND WHICH ARE BAD?

~ WHICH OF YOUR HABITS REGULARLY HURT YOURSELF AND OTHERS AND PREVENT YOU FROM ACCEPTING AND LOVING YOURSELF AS WELL AS OTHERS?

~ WHAT NEW, HELPFUL HABITS COULD YOU INCORPORATE INTO YOUR DAILY LIFE TO BECOME MORE CONSCIOUS, MORE HEALTHY AND MORE LOVING?

SMALL STEPS CAUSE BIG CHANGES ~

TRY TO PERFORM AT LEAST ONE SMALL ACTION EACH DAY THAT WILL TAKE YOU ONE STEP FORWARD ON THE PATH TO A MORE FULFILLING LIFE. ONE HOUR A DAY, TEN MINUTES A DAY, FIVE MINUTES A DAY: EVEN THE SMALLEST POSITIVE RITUAL CHANGES YOUR LIFE—AND THE UNIVERSE—FOR GOOD.

BELIEVE ME, STEP BY STEP YOU WILL BECOME THE PERSON YOU DESERVE TO BE, AND THAT WILL TRANSFORM YOU, YOUR FAMILY, YOUR FRIENDS, YOUR PRESENTATIONS AND THE WORLD AS A WHOLE.

GOOD HABITS FOR YOUR LIFE:

~ CREATE LITTLE RITUALS THAT GIVE YOU A FEELING OF HARMONY, LIKE MEDITATION, LISTENING TO MUSIC OR PRACTISING YOGA. (SOUL)

~ CREATE RITUALS THAT SHARPEN YOUR AWARENESS OF REALITY, SUCH AS READING, DISCUSSING, WRITING & PRESENTING. (MIND)

~ CREATE RITUALS THAT LOVINGLY CONNECT YOU WITH NATURE, ANIMALS & OTHER PEOPLE. (EMOTIONS)

~ GO TO BED A LITTLE EARLIER & GET UP EARLIER. BOOST YOUR LIFE ENERGY THROUGH HEALTHY & AND REGULAR EXERCISE. (BODY)

PLEASE NOTE: I'M NO MEDIC, SO BE SURE TO TALK TO YOUR DOCTOR BEFORE IMPLEMENTING PHYSICALLY DEMANDING CHANGES INTO YOUR DAILY ROUTINE.

"No man is an island, entire of itself, every man is a piece of the continent, a part of the main. If a clod be washed away by the sea, Europe is the less. As well as if a promontory were. As well as if a manor of thy friend's or of thine own were. Any man's death diminishes me because I am involved in mankind, and therefore never send to know for whom the bell tolls—it tolls for thee."

~ John Donne

Imagine being a celebrity known to millions of people, admired by students and internet communities all over the world and invited to talk shows and award ceremonies.

How would you act in public? Would you yell at the taxi driver, shop drunk at the mall or post words of hate on your blog? No, you would not, because you would be aware of the fact that you might negatively affect the behaviour of millions of other people on this planet by doing so.

You are a role model, too ~

Well, it is time to understand that you are a role model, too, because your behaviour influences the life of every other person who meets you, gets to know you or follows your presentation. Yes, you too are an ambassador of humanity, and you too should always act accordingly. This does not mean that you should never be nervous, tired or in a bad mood, but you should ask yourself what people around you normally take with them after having met you.

Does your behaviour help them to grow, develop self-love and love and become more confident? Or do you regularly make them feel small, bitter and hopeless?

LIVE YOUR VALUES ~

Always remember that your relationships with other people are the touchstone of your values and intentions. If you believe in love, you have to let it happen right here. If you long for peace, you have to work day after day on peaceful relationships. If you want to see more awareness and truthfulness in the world, you yourself must become more conscious and more truthful every day: at work, with your friends and in your family, but also with those who are unknown to you.

Your behaviour is like a wave that reaches far beyond your horizon and touches the shores of every man and woman on this planet. Your presentations are part of this unique wave.

LIKE IT OR NOT, YOU'RE CHANGING THEIR LIVES ~

Therefore live every single moment with this consciousness, speak every single word with this consciousness, present every single time with this consciousness: you are an ambassador of humanity.

"THE AUDIENCE WANTS TO KNOW WHAT THE WORLD IS LIKE AND HOW TO FIND THEIR WAY AROUND IT."

~ JONAH SACHS

MEANWHILE, YOU CERTAINLY KNOW WHAT I MEAN BY "THE WAVES OF OUR SOUL": THE AWARENESS THAT EVERYTHING WE IMAGINE, FEEL AND DO CHANGES THE LIVES OF THE PEOPLE AROUND US AND THUS THE HISTORY OF HUMANITY AS A WHOLE.

YOUR PRESENTATIONS WILL CHANGE THE WORLD ~

YOUR PRESENTATION IN A COMPANY, AT SCHOOL OR AT UNIVERSITY IS A GREAT OPPORTUNITY TO CONNECT WITH OTHER PEOPLE AND INFLUENCE THEIR LIVES POSITIVELY. BUT TO ACHIEVE THIS, YOU MUST HAVE THE COURAGE TO TALK ALSO ABOUT THE "WHY?" OF AN IDEA, PRODUCT OR SERVICE AND NOT JUST ABOUT THE "HOW?" AND THE "WHAT?".

WHY DO WE DO WHAT WE DO? ~

ASKING YOURSELF WHY YOU DO WHAT YOU DO IS A REALLY SPIRITUAL QUESTION BECAUSE EVERY QUESTION ABOUT THE "WHY?" OF SOMETHING IS ALWAYS ALSO A QUESTION ABOUT THE MEANING OF OUR EXISTENCE: DOES OUR LIFE HAVE A PURPOSE? IS THERE SUCH A THING AS A DIVINE FORCE IN THE UNIVERSE? IS THERE GOOD AND EVIL, AND WHAT DOES IT MEAN TO TRY TO BE AWARE, GOOD AND JUST?

THEREFORE, EVERY PRESENTATION THAT ASKS ABOUT THE "WHY?" OF SOMETHING WILL MAKE US MORE CONSCIOUS AND CLEAR ABOUT OUR VALUES AND GOALS AND THEREFORE ENRICH US ON THE SPIRITUAL LEVEL.

BUT OF COURSE, YOU SHOULD ASK YOURSELF—AND FIND YOUR ANSWER TO—THE VERY SAME QUESTION BEFORE GOING ON STAGE AND TRYING TO HELP OTHERS TO ANSWER IT.

TIP ~

CEO OF ENTERTAINMENT MEDIA PARTNERS AND TED-SPEAKER ADAM LEIPZIG'S FIVE QUESTIONS TO FIND YOUR "WHY?":

~ WHO AM I?

~ WHAT AM I PARTICULARLY GOOD AT, WHAT DO I LIKE TO DO?

~ FOR WHICH PEOPLE EXACTLY DO I DO WHAT I DO?

~ WHAT EXACTLY DO THESE PEOPLE WANT & NEED FROM ME?

~ HOW DO THESE PEOPLE CHANGE AS A RESULT OF WHAT I DO?

"MANY OF US SPEND OUR WHOLE LIVES RUNNING FROM FEELING WITH THE MISTAKEN BELIEF THAT YOU CANNOT BEAR THE PAIN. BUT YOU HAVE ALREADY BORNE THE PAIN. WHAT YOU HAVE NOT DONE IS FEEL ALL YOU ARE BEYOND THAT PAIN."

~ KHALIL GIBRAN

YOU WERE BORN INTO A VERY SPECIFIC FAMILY, IN A VERY SPECIFIC PART OF THE WORLD AND AT A VERY SPECIFIC TIME IN HISTORY, AND YOU HAVE GOT EXACTLY THIS BODY AND NOT JUST ANY OTHER BODY. YOU HAVE RECEIVED WHAT YOU HAVE AND WHAT YOU ARE FROM THE UNIVERSE WITHOUT HAVING BEEN ASKED OR BEING ABLE TO GIVE IT BACK:

~ SO, THE FIRST THING WE HAVE TO LEARN AS HUMAN BEINGS IS TO ACCEPT THAT ALL OF US WERE THROWN INTO EXISTENCE IN A WAY THAT WAS OUT OF OUR CONTROL.

~ THE SECOND THING WE HAVE TO REALISE IS THAT EVERYTHING THAT IS IMPORTANT AND VALUABLE TO US TODAY WILL EVENTUALLY WITHER AND TURN INTO SOMETHING ELSE AT SOME POINT IN THE FUTURE.

~ THE THIRD THING WE HAVE TO LEARN IS TO KEEP CONSTANTLY IN TOUCH WITH OUR ETERNAL SOUL AND THUS LET THE BEAUTY OF OUR BEING REACH BEYOND OUR DEATH.

BETWEEN OUR BIRTH AND DEATH—BOTH CONDITIONS WE CANNOT ENTIRELY CONTROL—LIES OUR FRAGILE LIFE SPAN WHICH HOLDS FANTASTIC POSSIBILITIES AS WELL AS TRANSIENCE AND DEATH. WE DO NOT REALLY HAVE A CHOICE: WE MUST FACE BOTH ASPECTS OF EXISTENCE AND WALK COURAGEOUSLY THROUGH ALL THE PAIN AND JOY THERE WILL BE, THUS DEFEATING DEATH.

DO YOU KNOW WHAT YOUR SOUL IS LIKE? ~

IN THE COURSE OF YOUR LIFE, YOU WILL, JUST LIKE THE REST OF US, LOSE YOURSELF MANY TIMES IN ANGER, DESPAIR, FEAR, GREED, SUPERFICIALITY AND ABSTRACT THINKING, BUT IF YOU KEEP BEING CONSCIOUS OF YOUR IMMORTAL SOUL AND

HER BOUNDLESS BEAUTY, YOU WILL ALWAYS FIND YOUR WAY BACK TO YOUR TRUE DESTINY.

FOR DEEP WITHIN YOU IS A "NOTHING" FILLED WITH SERENITY, PEACE AND UNITY WITH THE UNIVERSE. TRY TO CONNECT AT LEAST ONCE A DAY WITH THIS IMMEASURABLE AND NAMELESS BEAUTY WITHIN YOU. NO E-MAIL IS MORE IMPORTANT, NO PARTY MORE CHEERFUL, NO PROFESSIONAL SUCCESS MORE BENEFICIAL THAN THE NAMELESS PATH WITHIN YOU THAT LEADS TO ENLIGHTENMENT, LOVE AND PEACE.

THE ILLUMINATED PATH IS WAITING FOR YOU ~

DEEP BREATHING LEADS YOU ON THIS PATH, CARESSES AND MASSAGES LEAD YOU THERE, SILENCE AROUND YOU LEADS YOU THERE, BUT ALSO YOUR DREAMS, TAROT-CARDS, A PENDULUM, THE KABBALA OR THE I CHING.

AND IF YOU SHOULD ENCOUNTER MOMENTS OF IMPATIENCE, EMPTINESS AND PAIN ON YOUR JOURNEY TO YOURSELF, DO NOT BE AFRAID, FOR THIS IS AN IMPORTANT PART OF YOUR BECOMING TRULY HUMAN.

THE SUPPRESSED, NEVER CONSCIOUSLY PROCESSED PAIN THAT HAS ACCUMULATED INSIDE YOUR SOUL, MIND, HEART AND BODY OVER THE YEARS MUST BE ADDRESSED, EXPRESSED AND CLARIFIED, AND THE UNIVERSE WANTS—AND WILL—HELP YOU DOING EXACTLY THAT.

SO, LEARN TO CONNECT WITH THE WAVES OF YOUR SOUL EVERY DAY, AND ENJOY THESE MAGICAL MOMENTS OF ONENESS WITH YOURSELF AND EVERYTHING THAT IS.

IT MAKES LITTLE DIFFERENCE WHETHER YOU TAKE FIVE MINUTES OR AN HOUR TO DO THIS, THE IMPORTANT THING IS THAT YOU SET OUT EVERY DAY ANEW TO WALK THROUGH THE MOST BEAUTIFUL GATE THERE IS IN THE UNIVERSE—THE GATE THAT LEADS TO THE PARADISE WITHIN YOU.

UNFATHOMABLE, INDESCRIBABLE, NEVER-ENDING BEAUTY AND JOY AWAIT YOU THERE.

ALL YOU HAVE TO DO IS STEP INSIDE.

"KINDNESS IN WORDS CREATES CONFIDENCE. KINDNESS IN THINKING CREATES PROFOUNDNESS. KINDNESS IN GIVING CREATES LOVE."

~ LAOZI

Within every human community there is a cycle of love that ensures that we first grow and prosper with the help of others before we ourselves become a source of consciousness, growth and love for those who come after us.

MANY OF US HAVE BEEN HURT ~

Those of us who lacked tenderness, love and care in the first years of their lives may survive, but they will have to cope with the scars left by the loneliness they experienced on the surface of their soul.

Through the lack of affection and love, we humans become enemies to each other and to ourselves because to perceive life as a permanent struggle makes us inwardly hard and sick. We live and experience our days with a condom pulled over our hearts and thus contribute to the creation of a world in which loneliness, inner conflict, distrust, anger and religious fanaticism poison our coexistence.

So, what can we do in our daily lives to nourish the cycle of communion and to bring out the love that this circle creates?

WE MUST EXERCISE KINDNESS ~

The answer is incredibly simple and incredibly challenging at the same time: we have to practice in kindness every day.

The task is simple because we all remember how much we were grateful in our childhood whenever we

WERE TREATED AFFECTIONATELY, AND WE BASICALLY KNOW HOW IT'S DONE, BUT THE TASK IS ALSO CHALLENGING BECAUSE IT TAKES TRUE INSIGHT TO RESPOND TO INSULTS WITH UNDERSTANDING AND TO REMAIN FRIENDLY EVEN IN VERY STRESSFUL MOMENTS.

PLEASE DO NOT MISUNDERSTAND ME: TO PRACTICE KINDNESS DOES NOT MEAN TO GIVE UP LIVING IN ACCORDANCE WITH OUR VALUES, NOR DOES IT MEAN TO SUBMIT TO BLACKMAIL, VIOLENCE OR MANIPULATION.

INSTEAD, IT MEANS MAKING OURSELVES AWARE THAT EVERY OTHER PERSON, EVERY ANIMAL AND EVERY PLANT ON THIS PLANET DESPERATELY TRIES TO MASTER THIS EXISTENCE THAT NONE OF US HAS CHOSEN AND EVERY SINGLE ONE OF US STRUGGLES TO FULLY ACCEPT.

PUT KINDNESS INTO YOUR PRESENTATIONS ~

A PRESENTATION THAT MANIPULATES YOUR AUDIENCE THROUGH ONE-SIDED CHARTS AND ARGUMENTS CAN NEVER BE KIND.

A PRESENTATION THAT ADVOCATES GREED, SELFISHNESS OR HATRED CAN NEVER BE KIND.

A PRESENTATION THAT DOES NOT ASK FOR THE "WHY?" OF THINGS CAN NEVER BE KIND BECAUSE THE ULTIMATE "WHY?" OF ALL THINGS IS THE CYCLE OF LOVE AND THE KINDNESS IT FEEDS ON.

TO EXERCISE MORE KINDNESS IN OUR DAILY LIFE IS IMPORTANT BUT ONLY THE FIRST STEP BECAUSE WE ALL LIVE IN AN AGE OF WAR.

IN THE MIDST OF OUR DISSOLVING SUBURBS, SEMIDESERT SHOPPING CENTRES AND SOULLESS SKYSCRAPERS, A SILENT WAR IS RAGING BETWEEN THE FEW WHO ARE POWERFUL AND THE MANY WHO ARE POWERLESS, AND THE SAME SILENT WAR RAGES BETWEEN OUR CAT-GOLD CITIES IN THE WEST AND THE DARK SLUMS OF THE POOR AND EXPLOITED WILLOWS IN AFRICA AND OTHER PARTS OF OUR WORLD.

IF WE WANT TO SURVIVE AS A SPECIES, WE MUST CHALLENGE THE FEW POLITICALLY, CULTURALLY AND SPIRITUALLY AND FIGHT FOR MORE EQUALITY BETWEEN ALL PEOPLE, ALL CITIES AND ALL NATIONS.

IMAGINE! ~

To achieve this, we must broaden our concept of kindness and love and regard all other living beings on this planet as part of our family.

If we all act with kindness in our hearts all over the world and keep the well-being of all living beings in mind in all our decisions, the small waves of change may eventually merge into a surge of love, the whisper of understanding may turn into a symphony of compassion, and perhaps, at some point in the future, every child in the world may be able to fall asleep full and happy.

And then, finally, this world, now still torn and thirsting for kindness, will become one world.

"Injustice anywhere is a threat to justice everywhere. We are caught in an inescapable network of mutuality, tied in a single garment of destiny. Whatever affects one directly, affects all indirectly."

~ Martin Luther King Jr.

We all live in a magical and brutal, peaceful and broken, promising and hopeless world. Beauty, wisdom and love are not simply the opposite poles of greed, hunger and war; they are also penetrating each other, thus making it very difficult for us to decide where one of them ends and the other begins.

In other words, the reality into which we were all born is extremely complex and demanding.

We learn from childhood to find our way through this thicket of reality by looking at causes and effects, learning from these observations and adapting our own actions accordingly.

"When it rains, the road gets wet, and tyres don't stick as well on wet roads as on dry ones, so I should drive more carefully."

We call such a thinking "rational". Accordingly, we define "acting rationally" as the capability to use the right means to achieve a certain purpose.

Our so-called rationality is irrational ~

But why then is our world, in which we learn from an early age to trust this rationality, governed in the most irrational way imaginable?

Why then does our political system constantly create injustice and violence to which our government responds with even more violence?

WHY THEN DOES OUR ECONOMIC SYSTEM REWARD SHORT-SIGHTED THINKING, MONOPOLIES AND GREED, WHILE PUNISHING SUSTAINABILITY, JUST DISTRIBUTION AND COMPASSION?

WHY THEN DO WE HAVE A WORLD CULTURE WITH AN ALMIGHTY GLOBAL MARKETING LANGUAGE ON THE ONE HAND AND MILLIONS OF POWERLESS AND SPEECHLESS PEOPLE ON THE OTHER?

WE MUST REVIEW OUR IDEA OF RATIONAL ACTION ~

BECAUSE IT IS ABSURD TO TRAVEL ON PAVED ROADS ALONE IN A FIVE-SEATER WITH A COMBUSTION ENGINE, REGARDLESS OF WHETHER IT RAINS OR NOT, BUT THE FEW BENEFIT FROM SELLING CARS TO EACH AND EVERY SINGLE ONE OF US.

BECAUSE A PERFECTLY ORGANISED SLAUGHTERHOUSE IS ABSURD AND INHUMAN, BUT THE FEW PROFIT FROM OUR PITILESSNESS AND UNAWARENESS.

BECAUSE THE PRISONS AND CONCENTRATION CAMPS OF THIS WORLD ARE ABSURD AND INHUMAN, BUT THE FEW NEED THEM TO CONTROL THOSE WHO ARE AWOKEN.

TRUE RATIONALITY DOESN'T EXTEND ONLY TO THE "HOW?" AND "WHAT?" OF THINGS AND SITUATIONS BUT ALSO TO THE "WHY?".

TRUE RATIONALITY CONSIDERS THE LONG-TERM EFFECTS OF ACTIONS AND NOT JUST THE IMMEDIATE CONSEQUENCES.

TRULY RATIONAL ACTION LEADS TO DECISIONS THAT BENEFIT ALL LIVING BEINGS ON THIS WORLD AND NOT JUST THE 1% POWERFUL AND RICH, I.E. THE FEW.

TRUE RATIONALITY IS ALWAYS REVOLUTIONARY!

Chapter Two ~ The Waves of Our Mind

"Your presentation should not inform your audience, your presentation should convey meaning while dialoguing with your audience."

~ Phil Waknell

Nowadays, you no longer need to know when Napoleon won the Battle of Austerlitz, you just need to know where to find the stored information about this event, right? Or as David Brooks, columnist for the New York Times, once put it:

"I always thought that the magic of the information age was that we could know more, but then I realised that the magic of the information age is that now we can afford to know less."

Data in itself has no meaning ~

At first glance, this seems to make sense: our machines manage our knowledge for us, and we only use it when needed. Of course, we could also store the knowledge ourselves, but why should we?

The only problem with this argument is that data —facts, events, formulas—are not knowledge, and information, that is the data prepared and interpreted by others, isn't knowledge either.

In fact, you could possess records of the position of every atom in the universe, of all historical events ever occurred and of all books and essays ever written, and yet you would not know whether or not to greet your noisy neighbour, be jealous of your partner or punish your children for a lie.

Data does not in itself contain any meaning, and therefore it doesn't contain any recommendations for action either, and information contains only the interpretations and—sometimes—offers of meaning of others.

KNOWLEDGE IS US FINDING OUR OWN "TRUTH" ~

But what is real knowledge then? Well, in my opinion real knowledge revolves around the question of what is true, or better, what should be true for you, for me, for us.

Knowledge is not just storing facts, events and theories in your brain, but your own unique way of deciding what your life and the world should look like. Knowledge is your unique connection of hundreds of sensations, thoughts and visions to patterns of existence that only you can "see". Knowledge is a psychobiological, emotional and spiritual process that needs a soul, a heart and a body in order to succeed.

This is precisely why no computer in the world knows anything, and why the Internet, with its billions of hyperlinks, is per se completely meaningless.

For although a Wikipedia-article about Napoleon can be rewritten, reduced or enlarged over time, these changes will not change the character of the Internet because it cannot feel these changes, think about these changes and decide together with other living beings what these changes mean for its own actions.

YOU DON'T GO ON STAGE IN ORDER TO INFORM ~

This is a very important point to consider while preparing your next presentation. If your only goal is to inform your audience, don't go on stage. Instead, send people an overview, a summary or a link collection —as a basis for the actual discussion that will follow.

Go only on stage if you want to use data, facts and information to explore with your audience what is or should be true about a particular problem, what makes sense in a particular situation and what action is appropriate regarding a particular challenge.

Ultimately, knowledge is the result of an open discussion about what is true, what seems desirable to us and how we should act and live. Knowledge never arises in one person alone, but only in dialogue with others.

Become aware of the uniqueness of the medium presentation:

Canadian media scientist Marshall McLuhan (1911–1980) coined the famous sentence, "The medium is the message". Well, what is the message of a modern presentation accompanied by Keynote or PowerPoint then?

My—yes, somewhat funny—answer is: every presentation is a "time machine for knowledge tourists groups".

If there was such a thing as a time machine, then we would probably travel in groups & under the guidance of an expert into the future or past, and we would see stories, information, quotes, charts & photos on the displays of our helmets or pads while sightseeing places & objects, right? At the same time our "time tour guide" would discuss with us how the age we visited was a good or a bad one & ask us what our own impressions were.

I think that this exactly is the "message" of the medium presentation: we can exchange pictures, numbers & written words about any topic & discuss them simultaneously in the same room.

No other medium offers this possibility: neither cinema, television & video nor letters, telephone calls or e-mails.

"REASON IS FOUNDED IN INTUITION AND ENDS WITH INTUITION, LIKE A PAIR OF MASSIVE BOOKENDS."

~ IAIN MCGILCHRIST

WE KNOW THAT WE EXIST BECAUSE WE ARE NOT ONLY AWARE OF OUR ENVIRONMENT BUT ALSO OF OUR OWN EXPERIENCES IN IT. WE ARE AWARE THAT THERE IS AN "I" WHO MAKES EXPERIENCES AND THAT THIS "I" IS SOMEHOW IDENTICAL WITH US. DESCARTES' FAMOUS, "I THINK, THEREFORE I AM" IS NOT QUITE CORRECT IN THIS RESPECT. IT BETTER SHOULD READ, "I THINK, AND I AM AWARE OF THE FACT THAT I AM THINKING, SO I AM."

IN THIS CONTEXT IT'S IMPORTANT TO REMEMBER THAT CONSCIOUSNESS TAKES PLACE ON TWO LEVELS SIMULTANEOUSLY: WE THINK ABOUT WHAT WE ARE THINKING, WE FEEL OUR FEELINGS AND EMOTIONS REGARDING WHAT WE FEEL, AND WE OBSERVE OURSELVES IN ACTION WHILE WE DO SOMETHING. SO, WHAT WE USUALLY CALL "MIND" IS OUR THINKING, FEELING AND ACTING AND AT THE SAME TIME OUR ABILITY TO THINK ABOUT OUR THOUGHTS, TO FEEL OUR FEELINGS AND EMOTIONS AND TO OBSERVE OUR ACTIONS.

WE ARE MUCH MORE THAN COMPUTERS ~

THIS IS AN IMPORTANT POINT BECAUSE NOWADAYS WE TEND TO COMPARE OURSELVES TO COMPUTERS OR COMPUTERS TO OURSELVES. BUT OUR MIND IS NOT FORMED BY THOUGHTS ALONE, EVERY SECOND ANEW OUR "I" IS CONSTITUTED BY WHAT WE THINK AND FEEL AND DO.

THEREFORE, WORDS SUCH AS "SPIRIT" OR "MIND" ARE ACTUALLY MISLEADING, FOR THERE IS NO THINKING WITHOUT FEELING AND ACTING, NO FEELING WITHOUT THINKING AND ACTING, AND NO ACTING WITHOUT THINKING AND FEELING.

CONSEQUENTLY, THERE ARE NO PURELY INTELLECTUAL DECISIONS, EVERY DECISION IS ALWAYS ALSO AN EMOTIONAL AND ACTION-RELATED DECISION.

WE ARE EMOTIONAL BEINGS ~

A good example of how our mind is formed halfway between our thinking, feeling and acting is the way we create lasting memories.

The "amygdala region", thirteen small nuclei in our central brain, is a fascinating hub where our sensory experiences and the associated feelings and thoughts merge into memories.

All scientific studies about the amygdala region show that there is no lasting memory of events without the appropriate coding with emotions like fear, joy, surprise, sadness, anger, disgust or contempt.

That's why you always have to address your audience on an emotional level too, no matter how technical and rational the topic of your presentation may look at first glance. There is no lasting memory without an "emotional loading" of your facts and figures.

THE "NOWHERE MAN" AND HIS CAT ~

Just imagine this: in the head of every member of your audience sits a little "Nowhere Man" at his brain desk, and in his lap sits a big brown cat who is following your presentation together with him.

The "Nowhere Man" holds a big stamp in one hand and a small one in the other. Every time you show a chart with columns of numbers or a text-laden slide—and the cat gets bored and starts to lick her paw—the little stamp comes down. But whenever you tell a good story or show an extraordinary chart, quote or photo—and the cat begins to purr—the big stamp is used.

There is a third stamp, it lies at the back of the desk drawer because it is so rarely used, "This is going to change my life!" is what this one says. It lies there waiting for the perfect day, for the perfect presentation, for the perfect moment when the people in your audience will think, feel and do something they have never thought, felt and done before.

TIP ~

BECOME A CREATOR OF IMPORTANT MEMORIES:

There are three things that you should know about our amygdala nuclei:

First, they respond to the positive and negative impressions we receive during the day through our senses by causing strong positive or negative emotional states such as curiosity, appetite, sexual arousal & happiness on the one hand & fear, aggression & sadness on the other.

Second, the more intense the sensory inputs are, the more emotional markers the amygdala nuclei generates & and the greater the chance that a certain event will be remembered & become part of our long-term memory.

Third, the left amygdala region, which reacts more strongly to positive events, is larger & more developed in women, while the right amygdala region, which reacts strongly to negative events, is the main actor in the emotional learning system of men.

As a presenter, you should take this into account because men will be most likely emotionally triggered by warning of dangerous situations (the right amygdala), while women will react more likely to positive experiences (the left amygdala).

"IMAGINATION IS THE SOURCE OF EVERY FORM OF HUMAN ACHIEVEMENT. AND IT'S THE ONE THING THAT I BELIEVE WE ARE JEOPARDISING IN THE WAY WE EDUCATE OUR CHILDREN AND OURSELVES."

~ SIR KEN ROBINSON

Human growth requires learning, and if your presentations are to help people grow, then you should think about how we humans learn, right?

Put simply, we could define human learning as the ability to understand patterns of causes and effects by observing, interpreting and storing them in our imagination. In this sense, intelligence would be our ability to compare patterns we encounter for the first time with patterns we have already learned, in order to draw conclusions from the rules of those patterns known to us and apply them to those patterns we are encountering for the first time.

LEARNING IS ALWAYS "HISTORIC LEARNING" ~

But there is a problem: seeing a complex pattern of causes and effects and understanding how it works is only the first step. The second step is to ask the question of all questions regarding the observed pattern: "Why?". But, alas, we have been trained for centuries not to do that.

We call this phenomenon "culture". Culture is the sum of the meanings attributed to a particular set of patterns we call "society"—long before we are born into that very community. In this sense, our understanding of a fact is inevitably always part of a larger social interpretation of reality that points the way for our personal learning, so to speak, from the outset.

You might wonder what's wrong with that. Is it not an advantage to be born into a society that has already understood that a wheel rolls better than a

SQUARE? SURE, BUT THERE ARE NOT ONLY PHYSICAL, CHEMICAL AND MATHEMATICAL CAUSE-AND-EFFECT PATTERNS BUT ALSO SOCIAL, POLITICAL AND ECONOMIC ONES.

THUS, IN THE MIDDLE AGES A FARMER COULD BECOME AWARE OF HIS EXPLOITATION BY THE ARISTOCRATIC LORDS OF THE MANOR, BUT HE COULD NOT FREELY EVALUATE—THAT IS: UNDERSTAND—THIS FACT.

WHY? BECAUSE HE WAS BORN INTO A TIME WHEN IT WAS BASICALLY IMPOSSIBLE TO EVEN IMAGINE A WORLD WITHOUT RULERS, PRIVILEGES AND EXPLOITATION.

IN OTHER WORDS, A FARMER IN THE MIDDLE AGES COULD NOT TOTALLY UNDERSTAND WHAT IT MEANS TO BE A FREE MAN.

REAL LEARNING IS ALWAYS HINDERED ~

YOU WILL PROBABLY FEEL SORRY FOR THAT FARMER, NOW, BUT WHAT ABOUT OUR OWN POSSIBILITY TO QUESTION THE INTERPRETATIONS WE ARE PRESENTED WITH IN OUR OWN SOCIETIES TODAY? HOW DO WE LEARN TODAY? DO WE LEARN THROUGH A FREE AND CREATIVE DISCUSSION OF PATTERNS, OR THROUGH OBEDIENT REPETITION OF GIVEN INTERPRETATIONS ACCEPTED WITHIN—OR IMPOSED ON?—OUR SOCIETIES?

I JUST SMILED INVOLUNTARILY, DIDN'T YOU? WE ALL KNOW HOW WE LEARN IN SCHOOL AND IN COLLEGE TODAY, DON'T WE? WE DO SO THROUGH THE FORCED, ENDLESS AND JOYLESS REPETITION OF SO-CALLED FACTS: THE BATTLE OF AUSTERLITZ, THE PERIODIC TABLE OF THE ELEMENTS AND THE PRINCIPLES OF CYTOLOGY—ALL SPASMODICALLY LEARNED, SPAT OUT IN THE FORM OF CLASS TESTS AND FORGOTTEN THE VERY NEXT DAY.

WHO WANTS US TO REPEAT ? ~

IF WE COULD REGULARLY DISCUSS, RETHINK AND FREELY INTERPRET THE THINGS WE LEARN EVERY DAY, WOULD THIS NOT AUTOMATICALLY MAKE OUR SOCIETY MORE EQUAL, FAIRER AND FREER?

Right, but maybe that's exactly what she's not supposed to become? Personally, I think that the monotony of most presentations in schools, universities and academies today is not a "technical problem" resulting from the unprofessional use of presentation software. I think this dullness is the impressive proof that we do not live in a real democracy today.

The number of presentations around the globe, in which the dominant culture is creatively challenged with new ideas and approaches, is almost zero today. This constant and mostly fruitless reproduction of the generally accepted interpretation of social reality can hardly be a coincidence, wouldn't you agree?

In a time of mass consumption, mass media and mass politics the Few in power want to ensure that we come out of kindergarten, school and university with a lot of irrelevant answers and very few original and imaginative questions.

Our opportunity for a new way of learning ~

Fortunately, today's "turbo-capitalism" demands more and more creative, innovative and independently thinking team players, while the Internet, which has not yet been brought under control by the Few, is increasingly becoming a learning machine for new political and economic ideas.

The effect of this epochal change is that the power of the Few, that always was and still is based on the blind reproduction of "facts", is shaking today, offering us an historic opportunity for real learning and for finally creating a true democracy.

What our world needs are people who are trained from kindergarten-age on to interpret patterns freely, to discuss them fairly and efficiently with others and to try them out in practice—in order to be able to make socially relevant decisions that are good for us all.

Let this be from today on our true measure of any learning, and let this be also our true measure of the quality of our presentations.

"TOO OFTEN WE FEAR OUR OWN GREATNESS. WE PRETEND TO BE POWERLESS, MISTAKINGLY THINKING THAT THIS SOMEHOW FREES US FROM THE RESPONSIBILITY OF POWER."

~ STEVE PAVLINA

IGNORANCE, WAR, POVERTY, SLAVERY, HUNGER AND VIOLENCE AGAINST WOMEN AND CHILDREN—SO FAR WE HAVE NOT SOLVED A SINGLE PROBLEM FOR MANKIND. WE EMPLOY THOUSANDS OF MARKETING EXPERTS AROUND THE WORLD TO SELL SUCCESSFULLY YOGURT AND CHOCOLATE BARS, BUT WE CAN'T FIND SOLUTIONS FOR CHEAP HOUSING, AFFORDABLE MOBILE TOILETS AND DECENTRALISED ENERGY.

INSTEAD WE SPEND TEN HOURS A DAY WORKING ON A THOUSAND SMALL PROBLEMS IN OUR COMPANY, AND WHEN WE GET HOME IN THE EVENING, TIRED AND FRUSTRATED, WE KNOW THAT WE HAVE NOT ADVANCED THE WORLD AS A WHOLE. WHY? BECAUSE WE WOULD NOT KNOW WHAT THE REALLY URGENT TASKS OF OUR TIME ARE?

WE KNOW WHAT OUR WORLD NEEDS ~

NO, WE KNOW VERY WELL WHAT WE OURSELVES WOULD ACTUALLY NEED, WHAT OUR BROTHERS AND SISTERS WOULD NEED AND WHAT OUR WORLD WOULD NEED RIGHT NOW. THAT TRUTH IS IN US, BUT EVEN IF WE ARE WILLING TO RECOGNISE IT CONSCIOUSLY, ONE THING IS STILL NECESSARY TO REALLY TRANSFORM THE WORLD INTO A BETTER PLACE, MY FRIEND: OUR COURAGE TO ACT.

HOW OFTEN DURING A PRESENTATION OR SPEECH DID YOU FEEL THE URGE TO GET UP AND SAY: "ONE MOMENT, PLEASE, THAT'S NOT TRUE"? HOW OFTEN HAVE YOU YOURSELF PRESENTED DATA, CHARTS AND RESULTS THAT WERE CORRECT ON THE SURFACE, BUT ESSENTIALLY UNTRUE? "BUT EVERYBODY DOES THAT!" I KNOW, BUT DON'T TELL ME, TELL YOURSELF. BECAUSE DEEP INSIDE YOU HATE LIVING LIKE THAT, AND DEEP INSIDE YOU KNOW THAT IT'S WRONG TO LIVE LIKE THAT, AND THAT A LIFE AND CAREER BASED ON THIS KIND OF COWARDICE IS NOT REALLY WORTH LIVING AND NOT REALLY KIND TOWARDS YOURSELF, THE OTHERS AND THE UNIVERSE.

You may object, "I'm sorry, but at the moment I really can't afford to be honest. Not at this point in my life. Later, when I will have made my career and achieved my goals, I will begin to live the way I actually think is right, and then I will say what I really think."

Sure, but isn't that true of all of us? Who of us can just stand up and yell, "Wait a minute, not so fast!" without fear of consequences? None of us can, believe me. But on the other hand, imagine a world where each of us would stand up and say, "Wait a minute, that's not true!" if we were to nod off a lie.

It's time you grew beyond your excuses and took the power given to you by the universe. Trying to avoid disadvantages—a defining characteristic of our time—is cowardly and the opposite of personal power.

On the other hand, courageously accepting the pain and risks that await us on the path towards the truth is the greatest proof of your will to exercise your personal power for the good of all. For there dwells in truth a divine power, and if you commit yourself to it, you will live a more fulfilled life, helping others to become aware and thus changing the world.

Your presentations are important ~

We all need you, my friend, we all need your powerful ideas and your strong hands to hew stones of hope out of the mountains of despair that surround us, as Martin Luther King so beautifully put it in his most famous speech.

True hope only arises from truth, no matter how difficult this truth may be to bear at first. Security without truth is false security and the expression of a society in which we have given up our personal power to live a life based on pleasant but fruitless illusions.

Prepare your presentation with truthfulness in your heart, present courageously and powerfully and inspire your audience to courageous and true action.

That's what our world needs, and you know it.

"We are responsible not only for what we do, but also for what we do not."

~ Molière

The first step to a happier life is a basic realisation: you are responsible for your happiness. This does not mean that you should not discuss ideas with others, be active in associations and clubs and look for love. It simply means that you should take full responsibility for your well-being before you go outside to meet others.

Of course, this is the opposite of what you've learned all your life. Every pop song, commercial or political ad tells you that if you don't get this car, this man or woman or this product, you will be unhappy forever.

The problem is that almost all of us believe that happiness is about getting, and accordingly we are not very skilled in creating happiness ourselves by giving —and making ourselves and others more satisfied and happy in the process.

Imagine a world where everyone wants pizza from their fellow men, but nobody has learned to bake one. That's our world, and that is why we should become pizza bakers of happiness and learn to make a good pizza first.

You see, happiness is something that we have to create, feel and be, and by that I mean that we have to do all this during the one day that we actually live, right now, today. Living happily is an art form, just like loving and presenting consciously.

Become a master in the art of being happy ~

Therefore, you must first become an apprentice and then a master in the art of happiness.

Start by becoming an expert on your own body: what gives you energy, what makes you sick?

Also become an expert on your emotions: are there people and places where you feel comfortable? And who or what is taking energy away from you?

Become also an expert on your mind: discover which of your thoughts please you, and which make you unhappy.

Finally become an expert on your soul: what kind of connection to the eternal mystery that surrounds us satisfies you? Meditation, art, praying, singing, or dancing?

Experts are people who have tried things out. Try yoga, partner massages, running, cycling, praying, painting, meditating, opera, art exhibitions, movies, cookbooks, sauna and a thousand other things that interest you and do you no harm.

Take your time, choose the activities that suit you best and make them a positive habit, step by step and again and again.

Always remember: being good to yourself every day is not selfishness, on the contrary, it is the prerequisite of any true friendship and love-relationship that goes beyond mutual dependence.

The Few don't want to see you happy ~

Strangely enough, we are very rarely taught the art of making ourselves happy. Have you ever attended a happiness course in school, at university or at work? No? I don't think that's a coincidence.

Does our capitalist economy sell more goods to the happy people or to the unhappy? Are the happy or the unhappy people learning to live a deeper, richer and more fulfilling life with less? Do the happy people expect more from their government or the unhappy ones? What do you think?

Show them what their lives could look like ~

Remember what I told you above? Exactly, you're responsible for your own happiness. If you want pizza, learn how to bake pizza.

But of course, you should also help to create a society in which more and more of us become masters in the art of happiness and thus can experience and share more and more love.

Your presentations can help create that happier society, a world where we can all make our own, unique pizza and do not depend on that of others—but where we like to exchange pieces of it freely and with love.

Therefore, please, give out to your audience pieces of happiness, make them feel comfortable, make them smile, make them laugh, but above all: teach them the art of becoming happy in their own, unique way.

TIP ~

THE 5-STEPS-PRESENTATION-MODEL USED BY THE BEST OF THE BEST ALL AROUND THE WORLD:

~ IDEAL.
(POSITIVE)

~ REALITY—IN SHARP CONTRAST TO THE IDEAL.
(NEGATIVE)

~ REASONS FOR THE DIVERGENCE.
(NEGATIVE)

~ SOLUTIONS—VISIONARY.
(POSITIVE)

~ NEXT STEPS—CONCRETE.
(POSITIVE)

"THE WORLD WE CAN SEE WITH OUR SENSES IS VERY DIFFERENT FROM THE WORLD WE CAN SEE WITH THE ESSENCE OF OUR BEING. OUR SENSES PERCEIVE THE WORLD OF APPARITIONS. THE ESSENCE OF OUR BEING PERCEIVES THE DEEPER LAYERS OF REALITY."

~ PETEK KABAKCI

THE BASIC PROBLEM WE ENCOUNTER IN BUSINESS TODAY IS THE DISRUPTIVE POWER OF THE ROLES ASSUMED BY EVERYONE INVOLVED: MEET THE BATTLE-HARDENED KNIGHT, HEAVILY ARMOURED AND UNABLE TO EXPRESS EMOTIONS, MEET THE PLAYFUL PRINCE, SEEMINGLY IN LOVE WITH HIMSELF AND HIS DECISIONS, BUT IN REALITY INSECURE AND UNABLE TO CONTROL HIS EMOTIONAL OUTBURSTS, MEET THE UNSUNG HEROINE, OFTEN A WOMAN OF GREAT TALENT AND WORKLOAD WHOSE PERFORMANCE IS NOT RECOGNISED.

AS DIFFERENT AS THESE ROLES MAY BE, THEY ALL CONTAIN INSTRUCTIONS REGARDING WHAT WE HAVE TO SAY, THINK AND FEEL IN A CERTAIN MOMENT.

IN FACT, EXPRESSING OUR REAL THOUGHTS AND TALKING ABOUT OUR REAL FEELINGS IN THE WORKPLACE COULD SAVE US YEARS OF UNNECESSARY STRUGGLES, DANGEROUS MISUNDERSTANDINGS AND PROFESSIONAL FAILURE, BUT OUR FEAR FOR OUR CAREER IS GREATER—AND THAT IS WHY WE USUALLY STICK TO OUR ROLE AND TRY TO FOLLOW THE INSTRUCTIONS THAT COME WITH IT.

EXCELLENCE NEEDS INDIVIDUALITY ~

THE PROBLEM WITH ROLE PLAY ON THE JOB IS THAT IT WON'T LEAD YOU TO MASTERY. I LEARNED THIS FROM TENNIS. IN THIS WONDERFUL SPORT THERE IS A THEORY, ELABORATED IN DETAIL AND GENERALLY ACCEPTED, HOW A BALL SHOULD BE PLAYED, AND THERE IS—THE REALITY! THE TRUTH IS THAT NONE OF THE TOP PLAYERS IN TENNIS PLAY THE BALL AS IT IS EXPLAINED IN THE MANUALS. INSTEAD, EVERY TOP TEN PLAYER HAS HER OR HIS UNMISTAKABLE, UNIQUE PUNCH THAT PERFECTLY MATCHES HER OR HIS BODY AND TEMPERAMENT.

I find that interesting because after all we're all tennis players in the game called life, right? I mean, we all have to answer unexpected questions at the end of a presentation, respond quickly to an e-mail from an angry customer or at once comment on a business plan we're seeing for the first time.

Most of us do this in the one way that is accepted and expected in the organisation we work for, not in our own way. But the question is: Will this make us the Roger Federer of our company, the Maria Sharapova of our business field? Or will we always be the guy who plays on court 16, the girl who was considered a potential Wimbledon-champion at the age of eleven, but has never won a single tournament ever since?

I think that most of us do more or less well in what we do, but deep down in our heart we actually would love to become masters of our trade.

And why shouldn't we?

Looking closely, changes everything ~

That is why we are constantly thinking about what we could change in our work in order to become more successful. But tennis has taught me one fundamental thing about mastery: we don't improve primarily by thinking about which things and behaviours we should change, but by looking closely, by learning a new way of looking at things as a whole. Do you get what I mean?

Imagine being a tennis champion and waiting for your opponent's next ball: you know that this ball will have a specific length, a specific spin to the left or to the right and a specific angle before and after the impact, and therefore you look at the ball closely, and therefore the ball and its movements are all you see while you prepare your response. Do you understand? You look at it, you really look at it.

Becoming a master player is a side effect of your ability to really see every ball and its unique behaviour—and to react to it in a unique manner every time the challenge arises.

So, looking closely is a real game changer for your life as a whole and for your career in particular. The closer you look, the better you will become at what you do, whatever it is.

This, at least from my point of view, is the great secret you must understand in order to become a master of your trade. Now the question is: is business encouraging people to look closely today?

Looking the other way, kills success ~

I don't think so. Most companies keep their employees trapped in a network of strict roles and rules on the one hand and competition and fear of failure on the other. This type of corporate culture causes the loss of insight and promotes unrealistic fears as well as false expectations. People in such companies are afraid to say what they really see, think and feel about their customers, their products and services and their leadership. And usually they are pretty bad in predicting the market chances as well as the threatening disruptive innovations in their fields.

Say what you really see, think and feel ~

I think that, generally speaking, mastery begins with the courage to look closely and tell others about what you think is really happening around you.

It undoubtedly takes great courage to speak out uncomfortable truths in meetings, to discuss disrespectful behaviours of top managers and to renounce to "enhance" the data in your business presentation. But true mastery and lasting success—just like a truly fulfilled life and lasting happiness—are based on truth and authenticity.

Nobody has anything against tact and diplomacy, but sooner or later we should all be able to say what we really see, think and feel. This will not only help ourselves and our careers but also our companies and our world as a whole in the long run.

"A COMPANY'S GREATNESS IS GROUNDED IN DOING THE GREATEST GOOD FOR THE GREATEST NUMBER OF PEOPLE, AND THE LEAST HARM. IT IS NEITHER FIRST NOR FOREMOST ABOUT MAXIMISING THE SHORT-TERM RETURN FOR SHAREHOLDERS. RATHER, IT IS ABOUT INVESTING IN AND VALUING ALL STAKEHOLDERS —EMPLOYEES, CUSTOMERS, SUPPLIERS, THE COMMUNITY AND THE PLANET—IN ORDER TO GENERATE THE GREATEST VALUE OVER THE LONGEST TERM FOR ALL PARTIES, INCLUDING THE SHAREHOLDERS."

~ TONY SCHWARTZ

AN UNBIASED LOOK AT OUR PLANET SHOWS US THAT THE SUM OF ALL THE ACTIONS AND TRANSACTIONS CARRIED OUT, DEPRECIATES THE VALUE OF OUR EARTH INSTEAD OF ADDING NEW VALUE TO IT.

OUR WORLD IS IN PERSISTENT "OVERSHOOT", WE TAKE AWAY MUCH MORE FROM OUR PLANET THAN WE GIVE IT BACK, WE GET MORE OIL, FISH, ANIMALS, TREES, RARE EARTHS AND HUMAN ENERGY OUT OF IT THAN WE GIVE IT BACK BY HELPING ENDANGERED SPECIES, RECLAIMING DESERTS AND AIDING THE POOR AND AFFLICTED.

WHAT WE ARE GIVING BACK TO OUR MALTREATED MOTHER EARTH IS AN ALMOST UNIMAGINABLE AMOUNT OF WASTE INSTEAD, WASTE THAT WILL BE FATAL TO US AND OUR PLANET IN THE LONG RUN.

ABSURDLY, WE ARE NOT EVEN POISONING OUR WORLD FOR THE BENEFIT OF ALL THE PEOPLE ON THIS EARTH, BUT ONLY FOR THE 1% OF THE WORLD'S POPULATION THAT OWNS ALMOST HALF OF ALL WEALTH, WHILE A THIRD OF OUR BROTHERS AND SISTERS HAVE TO MAKE DO WITH LESS THAN TWO EUROS A DAY.

Losses are socialised, profits privatised ~

How could it come to this?

The main problem is that our current version of capitalism is a system that takes into account short-term effects, while it systematically ignores long-term consequences.

Fast profits made through the unscrupulous exploitation of people, animals and nature are not only permitted or tolerated by law today but, more importantly, also prove to be a competitive advantage in day-to-day-business. For example, the production of paper with the long-term poisoning of workers, rivers and surrounding cities as a consequence, gives a cynical board of directors an advantage over those paper companies that renounce quick profits in order to operate sustainably and avoid environmental pollution. Thus, the more nefarious company can push the sustainable one out of the market or simply take it over. This mechanism is in place all around the world while you are reading these lines.

But there is hope because today there is a global workforce of well-informed, globally connected and ethically demanding young professionals who are transforming the companies from within.

The "91s" will revolutionise our economy ~

These "91s", as I like to call them, are looking for well-paid jobs and strive for professional success, yes, but at the same time they want to live in a green and just world. They are willing to work smart and hard, but only if they also create added value for the world as a whole.

You may be wondering how this can change capitalism as a whole. Well, even the most ruthless companies cannot survive in a market where consumers are demanding green and fair products, their own employees want to remain true to their values and the top managers on the board want to look their children in the eyes without being ashamed.

ARE YOU ADDING VALUE, OR ARE YOU STEALING? ~

THAT'S WHY YOU SHOULD ASK YOURSELF BEFORE EVERY BUSINESS PRESENTATION: "DO WE, AS A FIRM, REALLY CREATE ADDED VALUE FOR EVERYONE INVOLVED WITH OUR PRODUCTS AND SERVICES, OR DO WE STEAL FROM SOCIETY?"

THIS IS AN INCONVENIENT QUESTION, NO DOUBT ABOUT IT, BUT IMAGINE A WORLD IN WHICH EVERY COMPANY, EVERY GOVERNMENT, EVERY INTERNATIONAL AGREEMENT AND EVERY MILITARY INTERVENTION, BUT ALSO EVERY PRODUCT AND EVERY SERVICE, WOULD BE JUDGED ON THE BASIS OF ITS LONG-TERM ADDED VALUE!

"THE RIGHT SOLUTION IS A PROGRESSIVE ANNUAL TAX ON CAPITAL. THIS WILL MAKE IT POSSIBLE TO AVOID AN ENDLESS INEGALITARIAN SPIRAL WHILE PRESERVING COMPETITION AND INCENTIVES FOR NEW INSTANCES OF PRIMITIVE ACCUMULATION."

~ THOMAS PIKETTY

OUR GLOBAL CAPITALISM IS UNDOUBTEDLY COMPLEX, BUT I AM SURE THAT MOST OF US COULD DESCRIBE ITS BASIC CHARACTERISTICS RELATIVELY QUICKLY IF ASKED:

~ POLITICS ARE DOMINATED BY LARGE CORPORATIONS AND BANKS. AS A RESULT, LARGE COMPANIES AND WEALTHY INDIVIDUALS ARE NOT OR ONLY INSUFFICIENTLY TAXED. TO MAKE UP FOR THIS, IT'S SMALL BUSINESSES AND PRIVATE INDIVIDUALS WHO ARE BEING ASKED TO PAY THE BILL.

~ GLOBAL PRODUCTION CHAINS ARE FACILITATED BY LOW TRANSPORTATION- AND LABOR-COSTS AND LAX INTERNATIONAL LAWS, REDUCING THE DIRECT COSTS OF CONSUMER GOODS AT THE EXPENSE OF WORKERS.

~ THE COSTS DERIVING FROM A DESTROYED ENVIRONMENT ARE PASSED ON TO THE REGULAR TAXPAYER INSTEAD OF THE LARGE CORPORATIONS: THE COSTS ARE SOCIALISED, WHILE THE PROFITS ARE NOT.

~ THE CAPITALIST REVOLUTION WE ARE EXPERIENCING TAKES AWAY MORE JOBS THAN IT CREATES AND DRIVES MOST SALARIES DOWN INSTEAD OF UP, AT LEAST IN THE WESTERN HEMISPHERE. THAT'S WHY WE EARN LESS AND HAVE LESS MONEY TO BUY GOODS AND SERVICES—WHICH THEREFORE MUST BE PRODUCED EVER MORE COST-EFFECTIVELY AND IN A MORE ENVIRONMENTALLY DAMAGING WAY.

~ THE SALES CRISIS RESULTING FROM MASS PRODUCTION IS FORCING CORPORATIONS TO MERGE EVER FASTER. IN THIS WAY, POWERFUL MONOPOLY PROVIDERS ARE CREATED. THESE THEN TRY TO CONTROL POLITICS IN ORDER TO EXPLOIT THE ENVIRONMENT AND THE GLOBAL WORKFORCE AT EVER LOWER COSTS, THUS TRYING TO SURVIVE THE VERY PROCESS THEY THEMSELVES ARE FIRING.

We all understand these connections more or less clearly, we all know that this kind of capitalism is doomed in the long run. The real question is therefore: how can we change course and prevent the "Titanic" from going down with us all on deck?

Economic growth can't solve our problems ~

It is obvious that we cannot outgrow this structural crisis of capitalism by delaying the collapse through ever more growth. Instead, we must finally take something away from those companies and people who have already accumulated too much.

We must redistribute the wealth that already exists, so that the billions of people on this earth, who have nothing, finally can get a part of the big cake.

That is why I think that all multinationals and all billionaires should pay taxes as well as pay fines for the long-term environmental damage they have done to the environment. That is why I think we should break industrial and financial monopolies around the world. That is why I think we should tax money transfers and close tax havens, and that is why I think we should put the mass media, the health insurance companies, the military industry, the waterworks and the energy- and internet-hubs under public control.

On the road to such global legislation, you and I should punish all those parties, organisations and companies that try to block this peaceful revolution for more equality and justice: by no longer supporting them, voting for them or buying their products.

One thing is certain: we must start acting as brothers and sisters if we want to change capitalism, not as Germans or Italians, not as Christians or Jews or as workers or managers. Our problems were and are caused by people and can therefore be solved by people, or rather, they must be solved by all of us before it is too late.

Your presentations will be an invaluable help to achieve this goal.

Start giving:

There is an easy way to become a "giver": give someone 15 minutes of your time each day to help him or her grow—without asking for money or any other payback.

At first glance this may seem very simple, but it's not.

Taking fifteen minutes a day to explain something to a person who is not part of your family, team or circle of friends, to answer a stranger's e-mail, to help a person in need or to go to the bank to make a donation, costs energy but helps to really change the world for the better.

And this will fill you with happiness every day anew.

"TO ATTAIN KNOWLEDGE, ADD SOMETHING EVERY DAY. TO ATTAIN WISDOM, REMOVE SOMETHING EVERY DAY."

~ LAOTZI

TODAY, I KNOW WHAT I'VE MISSED MOST MY WHOLE LIFE: TRUST IN THE FUTURE.

FOR MANY YEARS I USED TO BE VERY PROUD OF MY INTELLIGENCE, CREATIVITY AND KNOWLEDGE, BUT AT SOME POINT I REALISED THAT NONE OF THIS WOULD MAKE ME HAPPY IF I HAD TO LIVE IN MY BODY, HEART, MIND AND SOUL WITH AN AGONISING SENSE OF FEAR OF THE FUTURE.

THIS FEAR OF THE FUTURE STEMS FROM MY CHILDHOOD. MY PARENTS SEPARATED WHEN I WAS SIX YEARS OLD, AND I GREW UP IN A PLACE WHERE EVERYONE HAD A FATHER, EVERYONE BUT ME. I HAD PROBLEMS AT SCHOOL AND BECAME THE GUY NO ONE INVITES TO HIS OR HER BIRTHDAY PARTY. FOR MANY YEARS I FELT VERY ALONE, UNLOVED AND UNABLE TO FACE THE WAVES OF LIFE. UNTIL I FELL IN LOVE WITH MONIKA.

BUT MY DIFFICULT CHILDHOOD ALSO MADE ME AWARE OF SOME TRUTHS: FIRST OF ALL, I REALISED THAT THE BASIC YIN AND YANG OF LIFE IS NOT LOVE AND HATE BUT LOVE AND FEAR. THE MORE YOU LOVE, THE LESS YOU FEEL FEAR, AND VICE VERSA.

I ALSO UNDERSTOOD THAT OUR FOCUS ON POSSESSING THINGS AND PEOPLE STEMS ABOVE ALL FROM OUR FEAR OF LONELINESS WHICH IS ULTIMATELY THE FEAR OF DEATH.

I ALSO REALISED THAT FEAR LEADS TO RIGIDITY IN OUR BODY, IN OUR HEART, IN OUR MIND AND IN OUR SOUL, WHILE LOVE LEADS TO COMPASSIONATE OPENNESS, MENTAL AGILITY AND IN THE LONG RUN TO A CLEARER CONSCIOUSNESS.

TRUST IN LOVE, FOR LOVE NEVER FAILS ~

GRADUALLY, I BEGAN TO UNDERSTAND WHAT MY REAL PROBLEM WAS: FAR TOO LITTLE LOVE. MY THOUSAND FEARS HAD LITERALLY SQUEEZED MY ABILITY TO LOVE, AND WITH IT ALSO MY LIFE ENERGY.

WHENEVER MY PAIN OVER THIS LACK BROKE LOOSE—DURING A FIGHT WITH MY GIRLFRIEND, IN DISCUSSIONS WITH FRIENDS OR IN MY ROLE AS PROFESSOR—IT WAS, CONCENTRATED AND INTENSE AS IT THEN APPEARED, DIFFICULT TO BEAR FOR MOST PEOPLE.

I HAD NOT YET FOUND MY "BUTTERFLY POINT", THE POINT AT WHICH YOU LIVE ACCORDING TO YOUR VALUES BUT OUT OF A FEELING OF BEING LOVED AND BEING ABLE TO LOVE, THAT IS, IN A RELAXED, SELF-FORGIVING AND THEREFORE ALSO COMPASSIONATE WAY.

LOOKING BACK ON MY LIFE SO FAR, I ADVISE YOU THIS: TRY WITH ALL YOUR STRENGTH TO LIVE A LIFE THAT FEEDS ON COMPASSION AND LOVE FOR YOURSELF AND OTHERS, OVERCOMING FEAR OF THE FUTURE AND DEATH. DO NOT SEEK JOY AND LOVE IN EXPENSIVE THINGS AND ABSTRACT THOUGHTS, BUT INSTEAD ENJOY THE HARMONY THAT COMES WITH CLEAR, JOYFUL AND COMPASSIONATE CONSCIOUSNESS.

WAKE UP AND THEN CONSTANTLY NURTURE THE LOVE THAT IS AWAITING YOU WITHIN YOUR BODY, YOUR HEART, YOUR MIND AND YOUR SOUL.

A few things you can do to live a life based on self-love, compassion and love:

~ Take care of your body. Move a bit more, sell your car, buy a bike. Let the ones you love caress you & massage you. Enjoy your body & your sexuality & your deep desire for tenderness, love & care.

~ Change your eating habits, start enjoying the green wealth of the earth, stop killing animals for their taste.

~ Sleep more, dream. Write down your dreams.

~ Make time to feel yourself & all the beautiful possibilities that lie ahead. Take a deep breath & smile as often as you can. Face all feelings, even the negative ones. Sigh. Cry. Laugh. Try to Forgive others & yourself.

~ Enjoy this beautiful world, give away your TV & read and travel instead of watching others live their lives. Ride the waves of the ocean.

~ Dance, sing & make music. Be crazy for half an hour a day. Be courageous & playful like a young lion.

~ Help others as often as you can in as many different ways as possible, live a compassionate life. The happiness & growth of other people will make you happy & joyful, & it will help you to grow towards self-love, compassion & true love.

~ Most importantly: have faith in love because love never fails.

Please note: I'm no medic, so be sure to talk to your doctor before implementing physically demanding changes into your daily routine.

"SPIRITUALLY DEVELOPED PEOPLE, BY VIRTUE OF THEIR DISCIPLINE, MASTERY AND LOVE ARE PEOPLE OF EXTRAORDINARY COMPETENCE, AND IN THEIR COMPETENCE THEY ARE CALLED ON TO SERVE THE WORLD, AND IN THEIR LOVE THEY ANSWER THIS CALL."

~ Scott M. Peck

There are long hours of rain, magic evening hours and cosy autumn hours that invite us to think about our lives. We then look back on our years and ask ourselves—sometimes with fear in our hearts—what those things we have done and those we have not done will feel like at the end of our life.

What makes our life a success-story? ~

We might try to answer that question by recalling the number of dreams we have realised, the things we have built such as career, family and friendship, and the amount of joy and happiness we have experienced during the breathtaking moments of our lifetime.

I don't want to contradict that, all of that is important, but I think that satisfaction with life is also and maybe mainly about how much passion we do invest in working on the world as a whole. In my opinion, our amount of care for all the other people around us, or better, for all living beings on this planet, is our ultimate "Why?", and without it every "What?" and "How?" will feel superficial and unsatisfactory in the long run.

Can such high standards really be met? Well, sooner or later we all will have to cross the threshold that separates us from a life based on eternal, unconditional love for ourselves and for all other beings in the universe. The question is not whether there is an alternative but only how long it will take us to do it.

Live a passionate and generous life ~

Is that logical? No, but we will yearn in vain for enlightenment for a long time if we try to solve the mystery of our existence with our minds alone.

You see, logically, there shouldn't really be us or anything else in the first place, and yet we seem to exist. But since when? Since we were born? And will we continue to exist after our death on earth?

And why should we, thrown so brutally into an incomprehensible existence, also care about other people? Should we not instead try to use the few years given to us on this beautiful planet to realise our own dreams?

No, because only a wild, passionate and generous life will make us happy and befriend us with death. An existence as an "I" is lacking love and is unbearable in the long term, an existence lived within a "We", on the other hand, leads to happiness.

Only if—against all logic—we are willing to give ourselves completely to life and humanity, we will regain the magical essence of our existence, and only in this way we will end up looking back on our life with gratitude, joy and satisfaction.

"THE SCARY PART IS THAT MOST OF THE TIME WE MAY BE INFRINGING ON THE DREAMS OF OTHERS IN ORDER TO FULFIL A DREAM OF OUR OWN. PARTNERSHIP, PARENTING, MARRIAGE SHOULD REFLECT THE DESIRE TO HELP EACH OTHER BUILD FULFILLING LIVES FOR ALL PARTIES INVOLVED. YOU'VE GOT ONE LIFE (THAT WE KNOW OF). LIVE IT ... TO THE FULLEST!"

~ JADA PINKETT-SMITH

WHAT DO YOU WANT FROM LIFE? NO MATTER WHAT IT IS, YOU ARE NOT GOING TO ACHIEVE IT ALL BY YOURSELF.

YOU AND I NEED OTHERS TO FULFIL OUR DREAMS, AND THEY NEED US TO FULFIL THEIRS. YOUR DECISION TO BECOME PART OF THE BROTHERHOOD AND SISTERHOOD OF THE "DREAM HUNTERS" IS THEREFORE YOUR FIRST CONSCIOUS STEP TOWARDS A HAPPY AND SUCCESSFUL LIFE—AND A SUCCESSFUL, BECAUSE LIFE-CHANGING, PRESENTATION.

IT'S EASY LIKE THIS: FIRST THINK CAREFULLY ABOUT WHAT YOU WANT TO ACHIEVE IN LIFE, HOW AND WHY, AND THEN DECIDE WHETHER IT WILL REALLY HELP YOU AND THOSE AROUND YOU TO GROW.

NOW YOU CAN SPEAK OPENLY TO OTHERS ABOUT WHAT YOU WANT TO ACHIEVE, WHILE YOU WILL LISTEN CAREFULLY WHENEVER THEY TALK ABOUT THEIR DESIRES AND DREAMS.

FINALLY FIND THE INTERSECTION BETWEEN THEIR DREAMS AND YOURS, AND HELP THEM TO REALISE THEM AS YOU BUILD YOUR OWN FUTURE WITH THEIR HELP.

WE DON'T HAVE TO AGREE ~

A GOOD PRESENTATION SHOULD THEREFORE ALWAYS HAVE A "GOLDEN STARTING POINT", AT LEAST THAT'S WHAT I CALL IT. ALWAYS START YOUR PRESENTATION WITHIN THE PRECIOUS INTERSECTION BETWEEN YOUR INTERESTS, GOALS AND DREAMS, THOSE OF YOUR ORGANISATION AND THOSE OF YOUR AUDIENCE.

USE THE FIRST MINUTE OF YOUR PRESENTATION TO SHOW YOUR LISTENERS THAT YOU WILL HELP THEM MAKE THEIR DREAMS COME TRUE TODAY, THAT IS, SHOW THEM THE PART OF YOUR VISION THAT THEY CAN SHARE WITH ALL THEIR HEART. AFTER THAT, AND ONLY THEN, YOU CAN SHOW YOUR VIEWERS NEW, SURPRISING AND EVEN DISTURBING ASPECTS OF A PROBLEM—AND CHALLENGE THEM EMOTIONALLY, MENTALLY AND SPIRITUALLY.

BE COMPASSIONATE WITH YOUR AUDIENCE ~

THAT IS WHY, WHILE PREPARING YOUR PRESENTATION, YOU SHOULD ALWAYS ASK YOURSELF WITH WHAT VISION OF THEMSELVES, THEIR LIFE AND THE WORLD THE PEOPLE IN YOUR AUDIENCE START THEIR DAY IN THE MORNING. ONCE YOU HAVE THOUGHT IT THROUGH, YOU SHOULD CONSIDER YOUR AUDIENCE'S VISION IN EVERYTHING YOU DO ON STAGE.

THAT DOESN'T MEAN THAT YOU ARE NOT ALLOWED TO CONTRADICT THEM, ON THE CONTRARY, WE ALL GROW THROUGH DISCUSSIONS, BUT YOU HAVE TO RESPECT THEIR VISION EVEN IF YOU DISAGREE WITH IT.

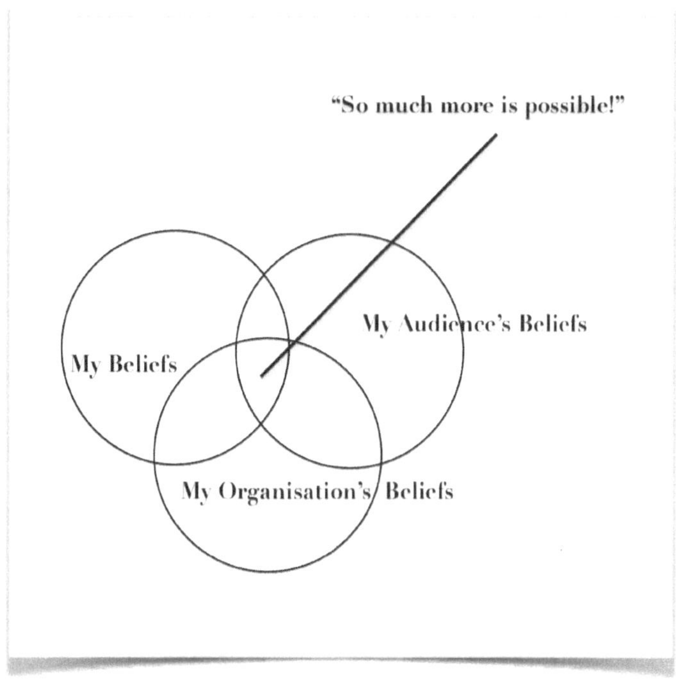

"If your actions inspire others to dream more, learn more, do more and become more, you really are a leader."

~ John Quincy Adams

The yin-yang between what is and what could be is probably the most powerful duality in the universe and the driving force behind every invention, every revolution, every search for meaning—and of course also behind every presentation.

But this power comes with a paradox that cannot be separated from it: the more our mind lingers in the future, the less we face the challenges of the present—and the fact that our "now", however terrible it may seem to us, is exactly the place where we must lay the foundation for Utopia.

Every big vision needs small steps ~

That's why our presentations must always contain both a big, inspiring vision and the concrete, small steps we can all take today to lead a better life, tomorrow. Our audience longs to contribute to a better future, to unite with the wave of positive change and to become heroes. They long to be remembered by their children and their children's children as those who have helped to save the world in one of its darkest hours, but they also expect concrete suggestions from you on how to achieve this.

We are with you ~

Deep in their hearts the people in your audience want to change this world just as passionately as you do, believe me. You are never alone, however unusual your own dream may seem to you.

Or as John Lennon once put it: "When you dream your dream alone, it's just a dream. When you dream it together with others, it becomes reality."

Chapter three ~ The waves of our body

"BE PROUD OF YOUR SCARS."

~ PAULO COELHO

THE GREATEST PLEASURES IN OUR LIVES—LOVE, ART, SEX, FOOD, SPORT, MEDITATION, YOGA—ARE ALL BODY-MIND EXPERIENCES, AND ALL THE GOOD AND BAD MOMENTS THAT TAKE OUR BREATH AWAY, ALL THE MOMENTS WE WILL NEVER FORGET, ARE BODY-MIND EXPERIENCES, TOO.

OUR BODY AND MIND WERE DESIGNED TO FORM A PERFECT PARTNERSHIP, BUT BOTH COMMUNICATE WITH US IN DIFFERENT WAYS: OUR BODY IS ALWAYS IN THE NOW, IT DOES NOT REFLECT ABOUT ITSELF, AND IT DOES NOT THINK ABOUT THE FUTURE. OUR MIND, ON THE OTHER HAND, HAS THE AMAZING ABILITY TO THINK ABOUT ITSELF AND TO WANDER BOTH BACK INTO OUR PAST AS WELL AS FORWARD INTO OUR FUTURE.

OUR MIND THINKS IT'S ABOVE NATURE ~

THIS AMAZING ABILITY OF OUR MIND TO REFLECT AND PROJECT MAKES US THE POWERFUL BEINGS THAT WE ARE, BUT IT ALSO HOLDS A GREAT DANGER: OUR MIND HAS LEARNED TO REGARD ITSELF AS ABOVE NATURE AND TO REGARD OUR BODY, BEING A PART OF NATURE, AS SOMETHING THAT MUST BE CONTROLLED IN ORDER TO FUNCTION PROPERLY. BUT OUR BODY WAS NOT MADE TO OBEY OUR MIND, IT WAS MADE TO RESONATE IN THE LAWS OF THE UNIVERSE.

OUR BODY WAS CREATED TO PULSATE TOGETHER WITH THE AIR, THE WATER, THE EARTH AND THE FIRE, TO PULSATE WITH DAY AND WITH NIGHT AND WITH THE FOUR SEASONS, TO PULSATE WITH THE MORNING AND WITH THE EVENING AND WITH THE MOVEMENTS OF THE STARS. OUR DNA IS THE RESULT OF THE NEVER-ENDING HEARTBEAT OF THE UNIVERSE, AND EACH OF US IS A RESONANT BODY OF THE UNIVERSE AND ITS CYCLES, AT EVERY LEVEL OF OUR EXISTENCE.

THE SEPARATION BETWEEN NATURE AND OURSELVES AND BETWEEN OUR BODY AND THE MIND IS THEREFORE NOT REAL BUT ONLY THE NARCISSISTIC WISHFUL THINKING OF OUR MIND. IN FACT, WHAT WE CALL "MIND" IS MINUTE PER MINUTE THE RESULT OF OUR THOUGHTS AND FEELINGS.

A "society of the mind" is dangerous ~

While our mind keeps telling us that it knows exactly what is good for us, we feel that its decisions force us into an existence where pain, insecurity and sacrifice are largely avoided, but that is superficial, boring and without any love.

We all are forced to live in a society where the awareness of the now is suppressed because it's not considered perfect enough by our scared and yet arrogant and tyrannical mind.

Our mind and our body are one ~

But our mind and our body are still one! Everything we constantly seek with our mind in the future or the past—happiness, joy, contentment, power, peace and harmony—are still as much body states as states of the mind, and the now, with all its unpleasant aspects, is still the only reality that exists and the only place where we can find all that!

Please take this into account while preparing your next presentation. You should always be ready to present with your whole body and not just with your head. You should always present with expressive hands, a vivid face and a passionate voice and change your position on stage dynamically in consonance with the structure of your content.

You should "touch" your audience by "emotionally charging" everything you say and show.

How? By starting your presentation with a stirring story, building an emotional bridge to your audience and subsequently show them strong contrasts, photos of real people and places, incorporating metaphors and rhetorical questions and repeatedly appealing to their hearts—and not just to their minds.

Our mind thinks it's above the body and its emotions. Whenever you present alone with your head, you are going to make the same mistake.

DISCOVER YOUR CHAKRAS:

"CHAKRA" IN SANSKRIT IS A WORD FOR "WHEEL" OR "TO TURN" & CAN BE DESCRIBED AS A PLACE OF YOUR BODY WHERE ONE OF YOUR LIFE ENERGY CENTRES PERMANENTLY ROTATES AROUND ITSELF.

THE SEVEN MAIN CHAKRAS FORM AN IMAGINARY LINE BETWEEN THE BASE OF YOUR SPINE & THE TOP OF YOUR HEAD, & FOR YOUR LIFE ENERGY TO FLOW THROUGH YOUR ENTIRE BODY, ALL SEVEN CHAKRAS MUST BE OPEN & ROTATING. ONLY IN THIS WAY CAN THE ENERGY OF OUR MOTHER EARTH, THE "PRANA", DIFFUSE INTO THE CAPILLARY ENERGY SYSTEM OF OUR ORGANISM, THE "NADIS", THUS VITALISING EVERY SINGLE CELL IN OUR BODY.

CONSTIPATED CHAKRAS AS WELL AS OVERACTIVE CHAKRAS CAN BE REGULATED BY MASSAGE, GENTLE PRESSURE OR CONTACTLESS STIMULATION.

DOES THAT SOUND ESOTERIC? TRY IT YOURSELF: HOLD YOUR RIGHT HAND A FEW CENTIMETRES OVER ONE OF YOUR SEVEN CHAKRAS & MOVE IT IN A CIRCLE OVER THE ROTATING CENTRE WITHOUT TOUCHING YOUR SKIN. FEEL THE ENERGY WAVES AS THE CHAKRA SPINS UNDER YOUR PALM. DON'T BE IMPATIENT, TAKE YOUR TIME. IN MY EXPERIENCE, THE EVENING HOURS ARE BEST SUITED FOR THIS TYPE OF STIMULATION.

"So long as we are in conflict with our bodies, we cannot find peace of mind."

~ Georg Feuerstein

If I should name a single metaphor that has accompanied me all my life, it is that most of us "sleep with their eyes wide open". When was the last time you drank a glass of water and really experienced it?

True experience needs a person who is present with all his or her senses, but we spend most days of our lives as prisoners of our thoughts: without really seeing what we see, without really hearing what we hear, without really smelling what we smell, without really feeling what we touch and what touches us.

We cannot create energy ~

But how can we awake from this twilight state and regain our full consciousness—and with it our passion, our liveliness and our love for life?

By remembering a basic truth that we have forgotten: all living beings depend on external energy sources such as oxygen, heat and water.

This energy, which we need in order to live, can neither be created nor destroyed by us, we can only transform it: in fact, we constantly absorb energy, transform it and then give another kind of energy back to our Mother Earth and all other living beings.

Take, transform, give back. Inhale, pause, exhale. Compress, become quiet and spread again.

That is the eternal pulse of existence, and we actually have only two possibilities: to pulsate in accordance with this eternal rhythm and to live to the fullest, or to block the resounding of this pulse within us and, as a result, to wither and die long before our time.

BECOMING AWARE OF THIS PULSATION OF ENERGY IN EVERY MOMENT OF OUR LIVES LEADS TO ENLIGHTENMENT:

~ WHAT WE CALL "TIME MANAGEMENT" IS NOTHING MORE THAN ENERGY MANAGEMENT.

~ WHAT WE CALL "RELATIONSHIPS" IS NOTHING MORE THAN THE EXCHANGE OF ENERGY ON A REGULAR BASIS.

~ WHAT WE DESCRIBE WITH WORDS LIKE "SUCCESS", "HAPPINESS" AND "SATISFACTION" ARE NOTHING MORE THAN STATES OF ENERGY.

~ WHAT WE CALL "PRESENTATION" IS NOTHING MORE THAN AN OPEN OR CLOSED CIRCUIT OF ENERGY BETWEEN YOU AND YOUR AUDIENCE.

OPEN YOUR EYES, OPEN YOUR HEART! ~

GIVEN THAT THE SOURCE OF ALL ENERGY IS DIVINE, YOUR PRESENTATION CAN BE SEEN AS AN INSTRUMENT OF THE HIGHEST BEING, THE VESSEL THROUGH WHICH THE UNIVERSE PASSES ON THE ENERGY YOU AND YOUR AUDIENCE NEED IN ORDER TO GROW. ACT ACCORDINGLY:

~ FEEL YOUR AUDIENCE, CONNECT WITH ITS ENERGY, BEGIN WITH YOUR PRESENTATION. BREATHE IN.

~ TRANSFORM THE ENERGY OF YOUR AUDIENCE, SHOW THEM SOMETHING THAT ONLY YOU CAN SHOW THEM, LET THEM THINK WHAT ONLY YOU CAN MAKE THEM THINK, LET THEM FEEL WHAT ONLY YOU CAN MAKE THEM FEEL. FEEL THE COMMUNION. PAUSE.

~ RECEIVE THE LOVE OF YOUR AUDIENCE, AND RELEASE YOUR LOVE FOR THEM. YOU'VE CHANGED THEIR WAY OF THINKING, FEELING AND ACTING, AND YOUR AUDIENCE HAS CHANGED YOURS. A NEW FORM OF ENERGY HAS EMERGED THAT WILL HELP THEM AS WELL AS YOU TO GROW IN THE FUTURE. EXHALE.

AND NOW OPEN YOUR EYES, AND BEGIN TO LIVE!

"BEFORE YOU ARE A LEADER, SUCCESS IS ALL ABOUT GROWING YOURSELF. WHEN YOU BECOME A LEADER, SUCCESS IS ALL ABOUT GROWING OTHERS."

~ JACK WELCH

Remember how we were as kids? We waved our hands to underline our sentences, our emotions moved visibly across our faces, the stormy clouds of anger as well as the radiant sun rays of joy, and in our voice resonated either deep sadness, or it vibrated with happiness.

But then came the dark years when we were forced to sit still in sterile classrooms and turn off our bodies. Our hands that wanted to fly, our legs that wanted to walk, our faces that wanted to express everything and our voices that wanted to scream, sing and laugh became prisoners.

So with each year that passed, we became more and more "man-machines", trained to live without connection with the wisdom of our bodies.

Thus we all were crippled in the name of a disembodied, emotionless and soulless "logic" that has proved so irrational that it has destroyed nature on this planet as much as our ability to feel deeply and to connect with other people in a loving way.

Therefore, if you want to lead us into a better future, you must first learn to reconnect your thoughts with your hands, your face and your voice—and become a powerful, passionate and authentic person again.

THE UNIVERSE WANTS US TO BE WHOLE ~

Integration, wholeness and healing: these words all denote a state of powerful liveliness, the very same liveliness that permeates every centimetre of the universe, the very same liveliness that can't but fall in

LOVE WITH US, THE VERY SAME LIVELINESS THAT LONGS TO PENETRATE US FREELY AND UNHINDERED IN ORDER TO ENLIGHTEN US AND MAKE US SHINE.

THIS POWER IS LIKE A WAVE WITHOUT A BEGINNING AND WITHOUT AN END, IT WANTS TO GROW, TO RISE HIGHER AND HIGHER AND TO REACH OUT TO EVERYTHING AND EVERYONE THERE IS.

THAT IS WHY LIVING IN HARMONY WITH THIS BOUNDLESS FORCE MAKES US SO POWERFUL AND SO CONVINCING ON STAGE: WHENEVER WE LIVE AND PRESENT OUT OF OUR DEEPEST HUMANITY, WE COLLECT, TRANSFORM AND PASS ON THE BENEVOLENT POWER OF AN ENTIRE UNIVERSE. A UNIVERSE THAT LOVES NOT ONLY YOU AND ME, BUT EVERY HUMAN BEING, EVERY ANIMAL AND EVERY PLANT THAT WE WILL ENCOUNTER IN OUR LIFETIME.

LEAD WITH HUMANITY ~

IT'S EASIER TO CONNECT TO OUR INBORN HUMANITY WHEN WE REMEMBER THAT THERE IS AN ETERNAL, INVINCIBLE AND YET KIND POWER ALL AROUND US THAT WANTS THE BEST FOR ALL LIVING BEINGS. IF THE UNIVERSE LOVES US AND EVERYTHING ELSE THERE IS, HOW COULD WE WANT THE OPPOSITE? THEREFORE, WE WILL ONLY ACCOMPANY YOU THROUGH YOUR PRESENTATIONS, BUY YOUR SERVICES AND PRODUCTS AND WORK WITH YOU IF WE CAN RECOGNISE A CORRESPONDENCE BETWEEN YOUR VALUES, YOUR EMOTIONS, YOUR THOUGHTS AND YOUR WORDS—AND THIS POWER.

THERE IS NO SUBSTITUTE FOR HUMANITY, THERE CAN'T BE, GIVEN THAT IT IS THE FOUNDATION OF EXISTENCE ITSELF. THAT IS WHY IF YOU LEAD PEOPLE BY PUTTING THEM UNDER CONSTANT PRESSURE OR BY EMOTIONALLY BLACKMAILING THEM, IF YOU LIE AND STEAL, TRY TO BRIBE OR EXPLOIT, YOU WILL NOT BE SUCCESSFUL IN THE LONG RUN, AND YOU WILL NOT BE FORTUNATE IN THIS LIFE. WHENEVER YOU WILL ACT WITHOUT HUMANITY, A WHOLE UNIVERSE WILL BE AGAINST YOU.

PASSION, KINDNESS AND UNIVERSAL LOVE ARE NOT EXOTIC OPINIONS IN A UNIVERSE CREATED BY COINCIDENCE, THEY ARE THE LIVING STAIRS OF THAT ETERNAL TEMPLE THAT EACH OF US WILL SOONER OR LATER ENTER.

TIP ~

YOU TOO CAN LEAD CHARISMATICALLY:

Communicating with your whole body not only makes you more human & more authentic but also more charismatic. This is the result of a research by John Antonakis, Marika Fenley & Sue Lichti in 2012 at the Faculty of Economics at the University of Lausanne.

According to this research group, we can learn & train charisma by using 12 "Charismatic Leadership Tactics", nine of which are verbal:

~ Use metaphors, parables & analogies.
~ Tell stories & anecdotes.
~ Use contrasts.
~ Place rhetorical questions.
~ Present only three features/ problems/ items.
~ Talk about your values & beliefs.
~ First, reflect the feelings of your audience.
~ Set yourself & others high goals.
~ Radiate confidence that goals can be achieved.

These are the three non-verbal CLTs:

~ Always speak in an expressive voice.
~ Express your feelings also through your face.
~ Pair your words with expressive gestures.

Antonakis, J., Fenley, M., & Liechti, S. (2011). Can Charisma Be Taught? Tests of Two Interventions. The Academy of Management Learning & Education, 10(3), 374–396.

Antonakis, J., Fenley, M., & Liechti, S. (2012). Learning charisma: Transform yourself into someone people want to follow. Harvard Business Review, June, 127-130.

Jacquart, P., & Antonakis, J. (2015). When does charisma matter for top-level leaders? Effect of attributional ambiguity. Academy of Management Journal, 58, 1051–1074.

"AND JUST AS THE TIDES EBB AND FLOW AND THE MOON WAXES AND WANES, OUR BODIES' HORMONES EBB AND FLOW AND OUR ENERGIES WAX AND WANE. OUR BODIES ARE MORE LIKE THE RIVERS THAN LIKE THE ROCKS, MORE LIKE THE OCEANS THAN LIKE MACHINES."

~ GOLDA PORETSKY

AT THE BEGINNING OF THE 21ST CENTURY, MOST OF US ARE LIVING IN NARROW APARTMENTS, ARE CRAMMED INTO COMMUTER TRAINS AND BUSES AND ARE TAKEN HOSTAGE IN TINY OFFICES AND CLASSROOMS.

SOMETIMES WE CAN FREE OURSELVES FOR AN HOUR OR TWO TO DO YOGA OR SPORT IN A FITNESS FACTORY, BUT MOST OF THE TIME WE ARE NOT MUCH MORE THAN SARDINES LIVING IN A TIN OF SARDINES.

OUR SECRET IDEAL IS THE MAN-MACHINE ~

OUR DAILY LIFE IS THE PROOF THAT WE HAVE ALL LOST THE PRECIOUS CONSCIOUSNESS OF THE CYCLES OF OUR BODIES:

~ EACH OF US WANTS TO STAY UP AND TIRELESSLY CREATE OR ENJOY SOMETHING, NOBODY WANTS TO SLEEP.

~ EACH OF US WANTS TO BE STRONG ALL THE TIME, NONE OF US WANTS TO FEEL TIRED OR WEAK.

~ EACH OF US WANTS TO LOOK YOUNG FOREVER, NONE OF US WANTS TO BECOME AN ADULT WOMAN OR AN ADULT MAN.

HOWEVER, WHETHER WE ARE AWARE OF THIS OR NOT, OUR FEELINGS AND THOUGHTS PULSATE IN HARMONY WITH THE GREAT CYCLES THAT SURROUND US. OUR IMAGINATION FLARES UP BRIEFLY, ONLY TO BECOME A FAINT GLOW AGAIN AN HOUR LATER. OUR CONFIDENCE WARMS US IN SPRING, ONLY TO COOL DOWN AGAIN IN AUTUMN. OUR FEARS ASSAIL US IN THE MIDDLE OF THE NIGHT, ONLY TO VANISH WITH THE FIRST RAYS OF THE SUN.

Our body is pulsating ~

At a time when the human machine—tireless, infallible and untouched by sorrow or love—is the secret ideal, this pulsation is regularly ignored.

The price we all pay for this idolatry is high. Just walk through a pedestrian zone for ten minutes, and you will see many people who have long since stopped hearing what their bodies tell them, what their hearts entrust to them and what their souls whisper to them. They are consumed and slowly dying, in a society that accepts this unnecessary withering for the sake of productivity.

We need a body-mind revolution ~

Learn to understand, respect and ride the cycles and waves that influence your life, your daily, weekly, monthly and annual cycles and of course your life cycle as a whole.

Don't go on stage in the early morning, not right after lunch or in the late evening. Shorten your presentations to twenty plus twenty minutes (presentation and Q&A), find the right moment for a sprint and the right moment for a break, give and take, express yourself passionately, and then rest again, find your unique rhythm, but in harmony with the universe surrounding you.

"THE MORE WE LEARN ABOUT TOUCH, THE MORE WE REALISE JUST HOW CENTRAL IT IN ALL ASPECTS OF OUR LIVES ... FROM WOMB INTO OLD AGE. IT'S NO SURPRISE THAT A SINGLE TOUCH CAN AFFECT US IN MULTIPLE, POWERFUL WAYS."

~ MARIA KONNIKOVA

THE DEGREE OF GENERAL AS WELL AS INDIVIDUAL HUMANITY WITHIN A SOCIETY CAN EASILY BE SEEN FROM HOW OFTEN AND, ABOVE ALL, HOW LOVINGLY PEOPLE TOUCH, HUG AND CARESS EACH OTHER IN DAILY LIFE.

THE LANGUAGE OF OUR SKIN IS UNIVERSAL ~

TO TOUCH AND BE TOUCHED IS THE ONLY LANGUAGE THAT EVERY LIVING BEING ON THIS PLANET CAN SPEAK AND UNDERSTAND.

OUR SKIN HAS A VARIETY OF SENSORS THAT CAN DETECT AND INTERPRET EVERY NUANCE OF TOUCH, AND THERE ARE A VARIETY OF BRAIN REGIONS THAT RESPOND IMMEDIATELY TO THIS PHYSICAL CONTACT BY CHANGING OUR BRAIN CHEMISTRY POSITIVELY OR NEGATIVELY: MAINLY BY RELEASING CORTISOL OR OXYTOCIN, SO THAT WE FEEL EITHER HARASSED, ENDANGERED AND REJECTED OR LOVED, PROTECTED AND PART OF A CARING COMMUNITY.

ELEPHANT BABIES DIE IF NOT TOUCHED REGULARLY, AND CHIMPANZEES THAT ARE NOT STROKED AND HUGGED, QUICKLY SLIP INTO DEPRESSION AND APATHY. AND THE SAME GOES FOR US HUMANS: WE ALL NEED LOVING TOUCHES TO FEEL ALIVE AND SECURE, HEARD AND LOVED, HELD AND UNDERSTOOD —AND TO GROW AND TO BLOSSOM.

SO, IF YOU WANT TO MAKE THIS WORLD A BETTER PLACE, START WITH YOURSELF: CARESS YOURSELF, FIND THE RIGHT PRESSURE, RHYTHM AND DURATION AND CARESS YOUR SHOULDERS, ARMS, FINGERS, HIPS, LEGS AND TOES AND ALL OTHER PARTS OF YOUR BODY. EXPERIMENT WITH MASSAGE OIL, AND BRUSHES AND ROLLERS IF YOU LIKE.

Become, be and remain "touchable" ~

I hope that in the future you will connect to your physical consciousness through your skin and be good to yourself, every day. Why? Because you yourself must become, be and remain "touchable" in order to be able to touch other people.

This also and especially applies to your presentations. People who have no connection to their body and their feelings go on stage and present from the head—and never really reach their audience.

Imagine you could instead communicate with people in such a way that they could feel every single one of your thoughts within themselves.

When a group of people connect in this way, harmony, compassion and deep understanding for each other arise. We could also call it "communion".

Rhetoric, as it is taught in most schools, universities and companies today, is nothing more than a manipulation technique, and it is no coincidence that the term "presentation techniques" is widely used.

The art of presenting is not a question of "technique", though, but your ability to touch and let yourself be touched by people—and to create that temporary community that makes mutual enlightenment possible in the first place.

FIND THE AMAZING "BUTTERFLY POINT" FOR YOUR PRESENTATION:

EVERY ONE OF US IS A GENIUS WHEN IT COMES TO TOUCH. WE ARE "SKIN PEOPLE" WHO CAN DISTINGUISH THE TINY DIFFERENCE BETWEEN TWO ALMOST IDENTICAL TOUCHES WITHOUT EVEN THINKING ABOUT IT.

WE RECOGNISE FROM THE INTENSITY OF A TOUCH WHETHER IT IS A FRIENDLY, DISHONEST, SPONTANEOUS, SEXUAL, CARING OR MECHANICAL TOUCH.

THE SAME APPLIES TO THE AUDIENCE OF OUR PRESENTATIONS. YOUR AUDIENCE IS EXTREMELY SENSITIVE, OR BETTER, IT IS EXTREMELY SENSITIVE IN TERMS OF INTENSITY: IF YOU LACK IT, YOUR AUDIENCE WILL NOT FOLLOW YOU, IF YOU ARE TOO INTENSIVE, YOUR AUDIENCE WILL NOT FOLLOW YOU ALL THE MORE.

SO, IF YOU WANT TO TOUCH YOUR AUDIENCE, YOU HAVE TO FIND THE "BUTTERFLY POINT" BETWEEN A "TOO MUCH!" & A "TOO LITTLE": BETWEEN TOO MUCH RESTRAINT & TOO LITTLE TACT, BETWEEN TOO MUCH AUTHENTICITY & TOO LITTLE COURAGE REGARDING YOUR OWN OPINION, BETWEEN TOO MUCH PERSONAL EXPERIENCES & TOO LITTLE STORYTELLING.

"Sometimes the more measurable displaces the most important."

~ Renèe Dubos

Your most important task on the physical level is to love your body.

To do this, you must master the most difficult challenge there is—accepting yourself. There is no love for yourself without first accepting yourself, just as there will be no true love for other people in you unless you have learned to love yourself.

Accepting and loving oneself as well as others happens above all in our body. We always become aware of this when we experience moments of love. Love always wants us to touch and feel who we love, to embrace and hold who we love, to be close to her or him who we love.

The temple of eternal love is our body ~

I have always been convinced that love permeates everything around us: the earth, the wind, the fire, the rain, as well as all the plants, the animals and the people. Our body is the channel through which this all-pervading love wants to transform itself into experienced love.

Unfortunately, our minds disagree with that. Moments of love in the here and now are not enough for our minds, they also demand the assurance of repetition in the future.

That is why we constantly think beyond the present moment, detached from our body which always lives in the now, and why we all too often argue and discuss where a simple embrace could heal us and others.

We can experience every day what happens when people dominated by abstract thoughts meet to discuss life without having ever acquired body consciousness:

POLITICIANS WHO HAVE NEVER SPENT A NIGHT ON THE STREET PRESENT THEIR UNKIND WELFARE PROJECTS, BROKERS WHO NEVER EXPERIENCED THE PAIN OF BEING CHEATED PRESENT THEIR DUBIOUS SCHEMES, STUDENTS WHO HAVE NEVER VISITED A FACTORY BABBLE ABOUT THE LAWS OF GLOBALISATION.

LEARN TO PRESENT WITH BODY AWARENESS ~

THE STERILE, COLD, RAZOR-SHARP THINKING THAT GOES OVER CORPSES IN THE NAME OF AN ABSTRACT IDEA ALWAYS BEGINS IN THE LACK OF LOVE FOR OURSELVES.

THEREFORE, IT IS NEVER A GOOD SIGN WHEN SOMEONE WHO PRESENTS QUITE OBVIOUSLY HAS NO CONNECTION TO HIS VOICE, FACE AND HANDS. IN THE BEST OF CASES HIS OR HER PRESENTATION WILL NOT TOUCH AND CHANGE ANYONE, IN THE WORST CASE IT WILL CAUSE UNNECESSARY HARM TO EVERYBODY PRESENT.

YOU AND I NEED TO DO BETTER ~

IMAGINE PRESENTING FROM YOUR BODY, WITH A LIVELY AND POWERFUL VOICE, WITH FLOWING, YET ELEGANT GESTURES, WITH STRONG BUT NOT HURTFUL MOVEMENTS, LIKE AN ENERGETIC, SELF-CONFIDENT, YET COMPASSIONATE WOMAN, LIKE A LIVING, SELF-CONFIDENT, YET SENSITIVE MAN.

IMAGINE HOW HEALING AND TRANSFORMING SUCH A PRESENTATION WOULD BE.

"Say who I am. Say I am you."

~ Rumi

We are all constantly connected: through our thoughts that effortlessly cross every matter, through our emotions that easily span the whole world all across the oceans, through our spiritual radiance that incessantly permeates the universe and through our bodies that share feelings with the surrounding bodies at every moment.

Our body is, strictly speaking, never our body alone: we see a person in need and immediately feel his or her pain in our body, we see joy on other people's faces and instantly feel their joy, we see pleasure in one look and suddenly feel pleasure.

The mirror neurones in our brain reflect the feelings of others by activating exactly the same nerve pathways that we use whenever we experience these feelings ourselves. This means that your feelings are always also mine, and that mine are always also yours.

Becoming connected is our destiny ~

The truth is that we are not separate people with separate brains and bodies but part of a large magnetic field of thoughts and feelings that, like the notes of a huge orchestra, create either harmony or dissonance at any given moment.

Just as a planet cannot stop influencing other planets with its own gravity and being influenced by them, we humans cannot choose whether we want to be a part of the psychobiological field formed by ourselves and the other people in space.

Of course we can ignore this field and its effects, but this does not dissolve the web in which we think, feel and act every day.

That's why we try to lose weight without considering that we are part of a network of people with specific eating habits. That's why we try to improve our finances without considering that we are embedded in a network of people with specific habits regarding money. That's why we try to change our fitness program without making sure that our friends and family go in the same direction themselves.

We all regularly behave as if we were only dependent on ourselves and then wonder why we keep failing with our well-meant initiatives.

Your presentation creates a magnetic field ~

Have you ever wondered why a flock of thousands of birds can perform complicated flight manoeuvres without one of them ever colliding with another?

They all become part of a magnetic field as soon as they are in the air together, they become one body, one mind, one feeling, one wave, and the result is breathtaking harmony.

Does all this mean anything to our presentations today? I think so, yes.

Do you remember the movies in which the bank robbers enter the vault with special glasses to identify the red or blue rays of the security system that are invisible to the naked eye? Metaphorically speaking, you should also wear this kind of glasses whenever you face your audience.

Who keeps in touch with the others in the room, and who sits alone? Who radiates goodwill and who rejection? Who is open to you and your ideas, and who needs more attention and convincing from you?

Once you feel the magnetic field that your audience creates in constant interaction with yourself, you can activate the unconnected, lifeless and loveless parts of your audience with your looks, gestures and words and integrate them into the field of your presentation—thus creating connection and understanding.

"YOUR EVERY LOVING WORD AND ACTION CREATES A FAR-REACHING RIPPLE EFFECT— LIKE THE WAVES OF THE OCEAN."

~ SWAMI DHYAN GITEN

You are the universe.

Every single breath you take reverberates in every place and sounds in every other person and every other thing.

So, whatever you do will inevitably make a difference in the existence of everything else.

Strangely, most of my students were taught exactly the opposite in school: "Whatever you have in mind for your life, forget it, you are not as important as you think."

So, my students come to my courses at university and present in the same way as they presented at school, they stage a sterile, abstract and mostly ineffective presentation in which they do not reveal anything about themselves.

In fact, they silently assume that nobody is interested in what they really think, feel and want, anyway.

MOST PEOPLE JUST FAKE A PRESENTATION ~

Do you understand this important point? Whenever people do something without being convinced that it actually makes a difference, their actions become a "do-as-if", a staging, a pro-forma action to satisfy the appearance.

Sad, isn't it? Yes, but that's exactly what happens when people's most important hope is taken away: that what they do will make a positive difference for their own future and perhaps even for the future of society as a whole.

Always present for real ~

You need to encourage the people around you to stop pretending like that. How? By demanding of yourself and others that every single presentation is aimed not at just informing us, but at changing our thoughts, feelings and behaviours for good.

Every presentation in this universe has, at the highest level, the purpose of connecting people and giving them the opportunity to enrich each other.

But we can achieve this only if each of us presents out of his or her uniqueness. Our lives are too precious to be wasted on listless and ineffective presentations by amateur actors.

You are this world, you are the universe, and everything you do—or don't do—changes the course of the world and the history of our universe. This is the boundless power at your disposal.

So stop pretending and get real.

TIP ~

PRACTICE THE ART OF BREATHING:

OUR BREATH IS OUR CONNECTION WITH ALL THE BEAUTY, WISDOM & LOVE CONTAINED IN AN ENDLESS NUMBER OF UNIVERSES, AND I CONSIDER CONSCIOUS BREATHING AS ONE OF THE MOST MAGICAL & SALUTARY EXPERIENCES WE CAN HAVE AS HUMAN BEINGS DURING OUR LIVES.

IF YOU WANT TO LEAD A MUCH HEALTHIER & HAPPIER LIFE & BECOME A POWERFUL SPEAKER ON STAGE, YOU SHOULD LOOK FOR BOOKS, VIDEOS, LECTURES & COURSES ON THE ART OF BREATHING.

THERE ARE A LOT OF CONCEPTS & IDEAS BUT I CAN'T MAKE THE CHOICE FOR YOU: YOU HAVE TO FIND OUT FOR YOURSELF WHAT SUITS YOU BEST.

PLEASE NOTE: I'M NO MEDIC, SO PLEASE CHECK WITH YOUR DOCTOR WHICH BREATHING EXERCISES & TECHNIQUES ARE SAFE FOR YOU.

"EVERY MORNING WE ARE BORN AGAIN. WHAT WE DO TODAY IS WHAT REALLY MATTERS MOST."

~ GAUTAMA BUDDHA

Today is the most important day of your life. It contains everything you can wish for, every opportunity, every possibility, every beginning.

Don't wait for a better day. This day is the best day of your life. This day is all you need to start your transformation.

THREE PRECIOUS STEPS TOWARDS A NEW LIFE ~

To gain more consciousness in your life, you can tackle three challenges on the body level: First become aware of what your body tells you throughout the day. Are you tense? And if so, where exactly in your body? Which areas of your body are warm, and which are cold? Which ones feel good, and which don't?

The second step is to find the right answer to your particular body condition: if you are hungry, eat, but do not eat too much, and try to do it slowly and lovingly. If you are tense in the neck, stomach or back, try to move and stretch carefully to relax your body in a loving way and make it supple again. When you feel tired and empty, take a break, walk and connect to the clouds, the sun and the wind until you feel energetic again.

The third challenge is to love your body more every day and to check your progress. Take a calendar and enter how many hours you slept, how much fruit and vegetables you ate and how much time you spent on your physical well-being.

In my experience, measuring small progresses without judging is far more successful than pursuing huge but unrealistic goals. "Kaizen" is what the Japanese call this approach that was originally invented in the USA.

Create positive rituals on all four levels ~

Of course, a good life consists not only of self-knowledge and self-love on the physical level, but also of your increased consciousness and the resulting well-being on the spiritual, mental and emotional level.

So, if you want to become a more conscious and happy person, you have to become a creative designer of your daily life by creating positive rituals of different kinds on different levels.

Think for a moment of all your negative rituals in general, like too much internet, too many cigarettes and too much loneliness. Have you really forgotten how many positive rituals are out there that you could celebrate daily instead or in addition?

How about training in the gym or taking a yoga class every day? How about spending time with your friends and experiencing tenderness with your partner every day? Why not turning off the phone and reading a good book? How about playing an instrument and singing and dancing and then meditating for half an hour?

The more you succeed in integrating positive rituals on different levels of your daily life and gradually abandoning the negative ones, the more fulfilled and happy you will become overall.

Become a true master of daily life ~

If you learn to ride more and more good waves joyfully, you will live better and longer—and deliver great presentations.

Sure, it may be years before you have become a true master of daily life, but the good news is that no one can stop you from starting this transformation right now.

This moment, as you read these lines, can change this day, and this day can change your whole life, and your new life can change our world forever.

TIP ~

TEN POSITIVE RITUALS FOR YOUR BODY:

- ~ GO TO BED EARLIER, RISE EARLIER.
- ~ TRY TO SIT LESS.
- ~ USE MORE SPICES & LESS SALT & SUGAR.
- ~ DRINK WATER, EAT MORE VEGETABLES & LESS MEAT.
- ~ GO TO THE SAUNA ONCE IN A WHILE.
- ~ HAVE (SAFE) SEX.
- ~ MEDIATE EVERY DAY FOR A FEW MINUTES.
- ~ KEEP A GRATEFULNESS-JOURNAL.
- ~ CARESS YOUR LOVER, & LET YOURSELF BE CARESSED.
- ~ WRITE POEMS, SING & DANCE.

PLEASE NOTE: I'M NO MEDIC. YOU SHOULD DISCUSS THESE ACTIVITIES WITH YOUR DOCTOR BEFORE IMPLEMENTING THEM TO ENSURE THAT THEY DO NOT HARM YOU & YOUR UNIQUE BODY.

"I must have a dark side if I am to be whole."

~ C. G. Jung

Do you have a dark side? Of course, you have, and so do I and everyone else. Where there is light, there is also shadow, where there is softness, there is hardness, where high levels of consciousness exist, there must also be lower levels.

The duality that permeates the universe and drives everything that exists, reigns also within each of us. Or as the poet Rumi once so beautifully put it: "We human beings can be pure as angels and as cunning as devils".

Do you know your dark side? ~

Do you know what annoys you, what makes you merciless, what triggers the worst thoughts, feelings and wishes in you?

If you want to lead a happy life, you have to face the dark aspects of your personality. There are no shortcuts, your mission is to become whole, and the way to get there leads past your dark side.

Don't get me wrong, this doesn't mean that you have the right to perform bad deeds, not at all.

Hurting others in any way is always wrong, and you should avoid it at all costs.

But to truly become a peaceful person in daily life—and not just in your imagination—you need to understand what awakens your shadow-personality in you, in which kind of situations that happens and how exactly.

In my case, I have realised over the years that the more I feel internally hurt and frustrated, the more I tend to hurt others. My shadow-ego apparently draws its energy from my feelings of being abandoned, being unloved and not being seen and accepted.

What's it like with you? Think back to your darkest hours: which emotional triggers bring on the kind of hurtful reactions for which you are ashamed a short time later?

Our shadows captivate us with energy ~

Do you remember how much energy was released in those moments?

In fact, our suppressed, dark energy initially generates a fascinating and apparently liberating force whenever we let our anger run free. But this destructive force doesn't really set us free, on the contrary, it damages our long-term relationships with other people and leads us more and more towards a lonely and sad life.

But what should we do then? Should we suppress the repressed bitterness, frustration and anger within us even more, so that no word, no gesture, no action can ignite and transform it into explosive rage? Should we repress all feelings of anger the very moment we become aware of them?

No, because many of us—especially women—have tried this road, only to discover that in the end it leads only to depression, loneliness and death.

The solution is another and, like all real solutions, it consists in a paradox: we have to accept our negative feelings completely on the one hand, but without acting them out immediately on the other.

Anger, sadness and fear are part of every authentic relationship with other people. But: to feel something and to accept this feeling does not mean that we have to act impulsively on the basis of this feeling.

Give yourself time instead to distinguish between short-term affects and lasting emotions.

If you learn to regularly cool down between situations that trigger your anger and your reaction to them, your life will change dramatically for the better. You will be able to live your negative feelings, but consciously and without any form of violence.

INTEGRATE YOUR DARK ENERGY ~

JUST TRY. POSTPONE AN OUT OF CONTROL MEETING BEFORE MORE CHINA BREAKS, WAIT 24 HOURS BEFORE REPLYING TO AN E-MAIL THAT HAS UPSET YOU, HOLD YOUR HAND BACK FOR A MOMENT INSTEAD OF POINTING YOUR MIDDLE FINGER AT THE DRIVER IN FRONT OF YOU.

SWEAR WHEN NO ONE HEARS YOU, BUY A PUNCHING BALL AND EXERCISE, OR THROW A WET TOWEL ON THE FLOOR A FEW TIMES WHILE NO ONE IS AROUND. AFTER THAT, YOU CAN STILL—AND SHOULD—TELL THE PEOPLE AROUND YOU WHAT MADE YOU ANGRY AND WHY. YOU CAN BE BOTH AUTHENTIC AND CONSTRUCTIVE-MINDED IF YOU WORK ON YOURSELF LIKE THIS.

IT'S HARD AT FIRST, BUT IT'S WORTH IT BECAUSE IT WILL TRANSFORM YOU FROM A HOLDER OF REINS INTO A REAL CHARIOTEER OF YOUR EMOTIONS, AS BUDDHA SO APTLY PUT IT.

DARK ENERGY IS SUPPRESSED LIFE ENERGY. SUPPRESSING IT EVEN MORE WILL KILL YOU IN THE LONG RUN. INSTEAD, YOU HAVE TO TRANSFORM YOUR DARK ENERGY INTO PROFESSIONAL PASSION, INTO ARTFUL DISCUSSIONS, BRILLIANT SOCCER GOALS OR GROUNDBREAKING BOOK WRITING.

THE DAY YOU REALISE THAT YOUR SHADOW-EGO WITH ALL HIS OR HER BLACK ENERGY HAS NO REAL POWER OVER YOU, BUT ON THE CONTRARY NEEDS YOUR WISDOM, YOUR COMPASSION AND YOUR PATIENCE, YOU WILL HAVE BECOME WHOLE.

YOU WILL STILL HAVE THE OPTION TO REACT AGGRESSIVELY TO OTHERS, BUT YOU WILL DO SO LESS AND LESS OFTEN, AND WHENEVER YOU ARE GOING TO DO IT, YOU WILL DO SO IN A CONSTRUCTIVE WAY.

YOU WILL LIVE AUTHENTICALLY AND COMPASSIONATELY AT THE SAME TIME—AND PRESENT AUTHENTICALLY AND COMPASSIONATELY—AND PEOPLE WILL TRUST YOU.

AND YOU WILL HAVE ACHIEVED ALL THIS NOT THROUGH THE SUPPRESSION OF YOUR DARK FEELINGS, BUT THROUGH YOUR TRANSFORMING YOUR DARK FEELINGS INTO CONSCIOUS AND THEREFORE ENLIGHTENED AND ENLIGHTENING ACTIONS.

CREATE SAFE PLACES WHERE FEELINGS CAN BE CLEARED:

Offer the people you lead & work with opportunities to spend time together & talk freely about their feelings. It is probably best if you drink a cup of coffee together every morning in a relaxed atmosphere & thus carry out a ritual of compassionate listening & sharing.

Our feelings are always there, & ignoring the negative ones will lead to nothing good in the long run. Feelings must be shared & cleared in an informal, friendly & relaxed atmosphere. Don't let negative feelings accumulate over days, weeks and years behind false kindness & staged indifference.

Give the people who are close to your heart & yourself the chance to clear your emotions every day anew.

"The unity and congruity of culture and nature, work and love, morality and sexuality, longed for time immemorial, will remain a dream as long as man continues to condemn the biological demand for natural (orgastic) sexual gratification."

~ Wilhelm Reich

Let's talk about sex, baby. Not about the shallow promise of sex, which is used to sell almost every product, but the real one that we would actually like and actually need on a daily basis.

My guess is that as a species we don't have enough sex today, or rather, we don't have enough good, satisfying and relaxing sex.

The liberating power of a climax, whose waves flow from one end of the body to the other, cannot be replaced by anything else, but who of us regularly experiences such an orgasm?

I think, in agreement with Wilhelm Reich, that this lack of orgasmic relaxation is one of the roots of the aggressiveness that we encounter all over the world today.

An uninhibited orgasm is a spiritual path ~

In fact, the moment we reach an unblocked, free-flowing climax, we can experience one of the great mysteries of existence: a moment without thought, where time ends and eternity begins. A free-flowing orgasm is perhaps the only moment in our lives where we are completely alive without thinking.

In fact, the sexual climax can be seen as one of the rare moments in our lives when we ourselves become existence: nameless and beyond every perception of time, of fear or intention.

Sex is thus a very physical and earthly but also a quite spiritual matter, and like everything else in this universe, it repeatedly gives us clues regarding the greatest mystery of all—love.

Love for yourself, love for your partner, love for all your sisters and brothers on this planet, love for your destiny, as tragic as it must be, love for this world with all its horrors and love for existence as such.

Sex can also work without love, of course, but as long as our sexuality and our ability to love do not merge, our orgasms will remind us that something is still missing.

Better sex leads to better presentations ~

Right now, you may wonder where the connection between sex and love on the one hand and the art of presentation on the other lies: well, most of the presentations given today relate to the art of presenting just like masturbation relates to the kind of sex that two people who are deeply in love have.

In fact, very few presentations connect those present in a loving way, and even rarer is the presentation that leads to an orgiastic moment of deep and free-flowing insight.

This is because most people who go on stage have not really integrated their sexual desires, their emotions, their ideas and their spiritual goals into a really balanced personality.

The fascinating thing about the art of presentation is that it can help us in this task: because it's true that you can only present convincingly when you have become whole, but it is also true that your progress on stage can help you to become an ever more passionate, lively and orgiastic personality.

"YOU MUST HAVE A ROOM, OR A CERTAIN HOUR OR SO A DAY, WHERE YOU DON'T KNOW WHAT WAS IN THE NEWSPAPERS THIS MORNING, YOU DON'T KNOW WHO YOUR FRIENDS ARE, YOU DON'T KNOW WHAT ANYBODY OWES TO YOU. THIS IS A PLACE WHERE YOU CAN SIMPLY EXPERIENCE AND BRING FORTH WHAT YOU ARE AND WHAT YOU MIGHT BE."

~ JOSEPH CAMPBELL

WE ALL WANT TO FOLLOW OUR OWN UNIQUE VISION OF OURSELVES, BUT AT THE SAME TIME WE LONG TO ENTER INTO DEEP RELATIONSHIPS WITH OTHER PEOPLE, WITH PEOPLE WHO VALUE US, CHALLENGE US AND HELP US GROW. SO, WE WANT TO BE EXCLUSIVE AND INCLUSIVE AT THE SAME TIME, BUT IT IS NOT EASY TO FIND THE FRUITIOUS BALANCE BETWEEN THESE TWO POLES OF HUMAN DUALITY.

LET'S TALK ABOUT POWER ~

WHY? BECAUSE WE'RE NOT FREE TO DO SO. EVERY OVERCROWDED COMMUTER TRAIN, EVERY FLAT THAT IS TOO SMALL AND EVERY AIRLESS CLASSROOM ARE PROOF OF THE POWER OF PROFIT OVER US, THE PEOPLE.

ALL THOSE ENDLESS MEETINGS, WORKING SESSIONS, AND HOURS SPENT IN SOULLESS COMMUTER TRAINS ARE AN EXPRESSION OF OUR ENSLAVEMENT FOR THE SOLE BENEFIT OF THE FEW.

WHAT CAN WE DO? ~

WE HAVE THREE OPTIONS TO RESPOND TO THIS POWER THAT INHIBITS OUR GROWTH AND WHICH IS BRUTALLY EXERCISED OVER US EVERYWHERE AND AT ALL TIMES: WE CAN CONNECT WITH OTHERS AND TRY TO CHANGE THE EXISTING ECONOMIC, POLITICAL AND SOCIAL RULES, WE CAN TRY TO BECOME MORE INDEPENDENT OF THOSE IN POWER OR WE CAN TRY TO BECOME A MEMBER OF THE "CLUB OF THE FEW" AND THUS AN OPPRESSOR OURSELVES.

In the first case, we must overcome our fears and our distrust and unite with others to create strong movements for equality, justice and peace—and our presentations can play an important role in this.

In the second case, we have to exchange our sports car for a bicycle, the TV for more time with our friends and a steak for more vegetables and fruit to become more independent of the Few and thus more powerful ourselves.

In the third case, through merciless self-exploitation and exploitation of the people around us, we will eventually try to become one of the Few powerful ones, but we will harm our body and soul and prevent ourselves from finding love while doing this. Because Karma is no joke, my friend.

We must exercise a liberating power ~

Whatever you decide to do in the end, you should develop a will to power because wanting to become powerful is not bad in itself, on the contrary, it is what we must achieve if we do not want to leave our world and our future to a minority of rich psychopaths. But we must strive for a liberating power, that kind of power that is based on truth, justice and brotherhood.

This quest for the liberating power of the Many is the eternal flame that has been carried from generation to generation among the greatest sacrifices in the midst of wars, poverty and injustice.

True enlightenment means being ready to receive this torch and later pass it on to the next generation—until one day we will all be free.

True enlightenment means clinging to the brightest and perhaps only hope we have as humanity—that one day we will all be ourselves, true human beings, and at the same time part of a truly compassionate community.

True enlightenment means knowing today that we will all one day be conscious beings capable of love.

FEEL THE POWER THAT IS IN YOU:

POWER ON THE PHYSICAL LEVEL IS—FOR ME AT LEAST—NOT THE ABILITY TO LIFT WEIGHTS OR RUN A MARATHON, BUT THE ABILITY TO CONNECT WITH THE POWERFUL ENERGY IN OUR BODY, DAY IN & DAY OUT.

THIS FASCINATING LIFE ENERGY FLOWS THROUGH US IN EVERY MOMENT OF OUR LIVES, & WHENEVER WE PAUSE, RELAX TENSE PARTS OF OUR BODY & CONSCIOUSLY INHALE & EXHALE, WE CAN FEEL THIS ENERGY VIBRATE WITHIN US.

SO, FEEL THIS MAGICAL POWER IN YOU, IT IS ALWAYS THERE, WAITING FOR YOU, BEHIND YOUR HURRY, BEHIND YOUR BEING TENSE, BEHIND YOUR TIREDNESS.

TAKE YOUR TIME TO FEEL THIS POWER AGAIN & AGAIN. LET YOURSELF "BE LIVED" FOR A FEW MINUTES, TRUST THE BIG WAVE OF EXISTENCE, JUST BE THERE & LET GO.

THIS TRUSTFUL BEING IN LOVE WITH EXISTENCE IS THE MOST PRECIOUS GIFT YOU WILL EVER RECEIVE.

Chapter four ~
The waves of our heart

"WISH I COULD BE A FRAGILE PIECE OF GLASS TO ACCEPT MY BROKENNESS."

~ MUNIA KHAN

At the beginning of this chapter on our emotions, I will tell you the opposite of what everyone else is telling you: stick to your fragility, to your ability to feel what you really feel, be it something pleasant or unpleasant.

You won't find many people, articles or books to give you this advice, and there are two simple reasons for this. The first is biological: our minds have been trained for millennia to look to anticipate dangerous situations in order to avoid them. This made sense in a world full of poisonous insects, hungry tigers and war faring tribes, but now our minds are doing their best to avoid any kind of unpleasant experience, such as disputes, separations or identity crises.

The second reason for the fact that fragility is not held in high regard in our society is cultural and interacts with the first: capitalism is not primarily the sale of goods and services, capitalism is above all a system based on the promise of good feelings. "Drink this soft drink, and you'll feel young and happy, drive this car, and you'll feel safe and respected, use this perfume, and you'll feel attractive and loved!"

In this sense, capitalism can be seen as the mass production of pleasant emotions, as the mass production of hope for a pleasant life without effort, insecurity and danger—and all the "bad feelings" associated with it.

SAY "YES!" TO EXISTENCE AND ITS DUALITY ~

That is why our minds as well as all the marketing agencies in the world suggest the same thing to us every day, "If you buy the right things and at the same time manage to banish all unpleasant thoughts and feelings from your life, you will be happy."

But this promise is hollow and will not make you happy because a universe without the possibility of "feeling bad" would be unsuitable to lead us to the most important feeling of all: love.

Being able to accept the duality of life as a whole—and the resulting human fragility—means to understand that the unpleasant situations and events and the resulting negative feelings are an important precondition for our spiritual growth.

Therefore, my dear reader, the following part of my book will be a plea for fragility, for a life full of tragedy, struggle, growth and love.

You know, whenever I am asked what makes a person on stage charismatic and his or her presentation outstanding, one of my favourite expressions comes to my mind: "hard hope".

Whenever someone of us is able to speak words of hope that come from a heart that is gone through hard times and tough experiences without ever surrendering to hate and bitterness, we are inspired to hold on to this difficult, tragic and yet beautiful life.

Seeing life in its tragic totality, really, and yet holding on to our fragility and humanity, makes us inspiring beyond imagination.

Accept life and inspire others ~

People who have only experienced birthday parties, basketball matches and VIP-dinners don't have much to say, in life or on stage. Those among us who have gone wild, who have tried and failed, who have been rejected and hurt and yet—or for that very reason?—have become even more generous, patient and compassionate, are those who touch us, in life and on stage.

Because to have accepted our own fragility while tenaciously holding on to our dreams means to have understood everything.

TIP ~

PRACTICE DIVERSITY:

WORKING WITH PEOPLE WHO CHERISH A DIFFERENT CULTURE, RELIGION, SEXUAL ORIENTATION OR POLITICAL IDEA REQUIRES CONTINUOUS & SOMETIMES TIME-CONSUMING LEARNING & CONFRONTS US WITH DOUBTS & QUESTIONS ABOUT OUR OWN LIFE PLAN. BUT LEARNING TO DEAL WITH DIVERSITY IS NOT ONLY A PREREQUISITE FOR COMPASSION & TRUE DEMOCRACY, BUT ALSO FOR YOUR PERSONAL SUCCESS, ESPECIALLY IN THE ART OF PRESENTATION.

TODAY WE LIVE IN A WORLD IN WHICH MIGRANTS, WOMEN, PEOPLE WITH FUNCTIONAL IMPAIRMENTS & OTHER IMPORTANT GROUPS IN SOCIETY ARE QUITE RIGHTLY FIGHTING FOR MORE RESPECT, INDEPENDENCE & EQUALITY.

CONSCIOUSLY CHOOSING ONLY THOSE TERMS, SYMBOLS & STORIES FOR OUR PRESENTATIONS THAT DO NOT DEVALUE ANYONE IN OUR AUDIENCE, WILL ENABLE US TO WIN MORE SUPPORT, TO GET MORE & MORE CREATIVE INPUT FROM EVERYONE & TO BE MORE SUCCESSFUL IN THE LONG RUN.

BUT ABOVE ALL: PRACTISING DIVERSITY WITH CONVICTION AFTER HAVING LEARNED TO SEE IT AS A CHANCE FOR ENRICHMENT IS A SURE SIGN THAT YOU HAVE LEARNED TO SAY "YES!" TO LIFE WITH ALL ITS BEAUTIFUL COLOURS.

"ALL OUR EMOTIONS ARE REAL, BUT ONE HAS TO BE QUITE CAUTIOUS WITH WHAT SUPPORTS THEIR REALITY."

~ ALEKSANDRA NINKOVIC

HOW ARE YOU FEELING RIGHT NOW? HARD TO SAY?

WELL, THEN THE FACT THAT NEUROBIOLOGY, SOCIOLOGY AND LINGUISTICS ARE NOT MUCH BETTER AT DESCRIBING EMOTIONS THAN YOU MIGHT COMFORT YOU. IN FACT, THEY DEFINE AN EMOTION AS "AN ACTIVITY PATTERN IN OUR BODY THAT OCCURS WHEN WE RESPOND TO A POSITIVE OR NEGATIVE EXPERIENCE", AND THAT DOES NOT CARRY US VERY FAR, RIGHT? FOR WHAT EXPERIENCE IS TO BE REGARDED AS "POSITIVE" AND WHAT AS "NEGATIVE" IS NOT AN OBJECTIVE MATTER.

IN FACT, WE ARE ALL BORN INTO A CULTURAL FRAMEWORK THAT DETERMINES THE FEELINGS WITH WHICH WE ARE EXPECTED TO REACT TO A CERTAIN SITUATION. IF YOU WIPE YOUR NOSE WITH A HANDKERCHIEF IN TOKYO, IT WILL CAUSE A FEELING OF DISGUST IN THE SURROUNDING JAPANESE, WHILE THE PEOPLE IN HAMBURG OR PARIS WILL HARDLY REACT NEGATIVELY TO IT, IF THEY REACT AT ALL.

ALTHOUGH THE SOCIAL SITUATION IS THE SAME IN BOTH CASES, THE JAPANESE AND GERMANS HAVE APPARENTLY "LEARNED" TO CONNECT VERY DIFFERENT EMOTIONS WITH IT ON THE BASIS OF THEIR RESPECTIVE CULTURES. BUT, AND THIS IS THE INTERESTING FACT HERE, TO THE PEOPLE IN BOTH COUNTRIES THEIR RESPECTIVE, OPPOSITE EMOTIONS WILL APPEAR TO BE "SPONTANEOUS", "NATURAL" AND "NORMAL".

THERE ARE AT LEAST THREE TYPES OF EMOTIONS ~

OUR EMOTIONS ARE THEREFORE NOT AS "UNIVERSAL" AS THEY INITIALLY APPEAR TO US, BUT ALWAYS ALSO AN EXPRESSION OF THE SOCIAL CONDITIONS INTO WHICH WE WERE BORN. THEY ARE "CONSTRUCTED". BUT, AND THIS DOES NOT NECESSARILY MAKE IT EASIER TO UNDERSTAND OUR FEELINGS, THERE ARE ACTUALLY ALSO EMOTIONS THAT ARE LESS CULTURALLY DETERMINED AND THEREFORE MORE UNIVERSAL:

~ Basic emotions that are directly triggered by the basic needs of our body, such as thirst, hunger or lack of physical contact.

~ Mirrored emotions, such as anger, joy, surprise, disgust, fear and sadness, triggered by the firing of the mirror neurones in our brain whenever we observe someone who experiences these feelings.

So, the reason why it is so difficult to understand yourself and others stems from the fact that constructed, mirrored and basic emotions intermingle and influence each other constantly.

Keeping a diary and writing down the events of the day and your feelings connected to them is one of the many ways to find out in which occasions you are experiencing certain feelings and why.

Emotions are real but not always true ~

Recognising your own emotional patterns will help you to take the reality of your inner world seriously, but not to confuse it with the reality of your outer world. Because although our feelings are always real, they are not always true.

If, as soon as I board a plane, I experience the feeling that I am in great danger, it is good to be aware of this and to remind myself with a wink that statistically speaking I have already put the greatest danger—namely the journey to the airport—behind me.

Your audience should do the same, it should be able to differentiate between "personal reality" and "independent reality", but don't count on it. Your audience will bring feelings into your presentation and project them onto you. In fact, some women and men in your audience will reject you, while others will like you even before you have said your first sentence.

Be emotionally prepared, keep smiling and don't become the slave of the mixed feelings, false expectations and unrealistic projections of your audience. Follow your game plan and win them over with your own conscious, positive and unswerving emotions.

USE YOUR KNOWLEDGE OF THE THREE TYPES OF EMOTIONS:

~ WHENEVER POSSIBLE, CREATE A POSITIVE ATMOSPHERE IN THE RUN-UP TO YOUR PRESENTATION: ENSURE GOOD AIR, THE RIGHT TEMPERATURE & THE RIGHT LIGHT. (BASIC EMOTIONS)

~ TRY TO EXPRESS CONSCIOUSLY WITH YOUR FACE, VOICE & GESTURES WHAT YOUR AUDIENCE SHOULD FEEL THROUGHOUT YOUR PRESENTATION. (REFLECTED EMOTIONS)

~ USE EMOTIONALLY CHARGED PHOTOS DURING YOUR PRESENTATION THAT TRIGGER EXACTLY THE SOCIALLY CONSTRUCTED FEELINGS YOU NEED FOR YOUR ARGUMENT. (CONSTRUCTED EMOTIONS)

THE PEOPLE IN YOUR AUDIENCE MAY EVENTUALLY FORGET WHAT YOU SAID TO THEM, BUT THEY WILL ALWAYS REMEMBER WHAT YOU MADE THEM FEEL DURING YOUR OUTSTANDING PRESENTATION.

"UNCERTAINTY, IF WE CAN TOLERATE IT, DRIVES US TO LEARN MORE AND CONNECT TO ONE ANOTHER; IT MAKES US SMARTER AND MORE COMPASSIONATE. BUT THE TODDLER BRAIN CANNOT TOLERATE UNCERTAINTY BECAUSE IT PROVOKES TOO MUCH ANXIETY."

~ STEVEN STOSNY

"I WANT THE SUN TO SHINE FOR ME AT ALL TIMES, I WANT TO DO ANYTHING WITHOUT BEING TO BLAME FOR ANYTHING AND I WANT MY FELLOW HUMAN ALWAYS READY TO GIVE ME EXACTLY WHAT I NEED WHEN I NEED IT."

DOES THIS ATTITUDE TOWARDS LIFE SOUND FAMILIAR? OF COURSE, BECAUSE YOU HAVE BEEN THROUGH THIS PERIOD OF DEVELOPMENT AS SURE AS I HAVE. AS YOUNG CHILDREN, WE WERE ALL CONVINCED THAT EVERYTHING AND EVERYONE WAS THERE TO MAKE US HAPPY.

ACCORDINGLY, IF OUR PARENTS DIDN'T WANT US TO KICK OUR PRINCELY FEET AROUND US, SHOUT OR THROW THINGS THROUGH THE ROOM, THEY HAD TO DELIVER WHAT WE WANTED, AND THEY HAD TO DO SO IMMEDIATELY.

I STRESSED THE WORD "IMMEDIATELY" BECAUSE AS TODDLERS WE WERE NOT ONLY MERCILESS ALL-OR-NOTHING-DESPOTS BUT ALSO PASSIONATE NOW-OR-NEVER-TYRANTS.

HOW MANY OF US ARE REAL ADULTS? ~

HOW MANY PEOPLE DO YOU KNOW WHO HAVE OVERCOME THE CLASSIC TODDLER MECHANISMS THAT STEVEN STOSNY LISTS: DENYING RESPONSIBILITY, BLAMING OTHERS AND AVOIDING INSECURITY? NOT THAT MANY, RIGHT? AND EVEN MORE RARELY DO WE MEET PEOPLE WHO CAN ACCEPT THE POSTPONEMENT OF SATISFACTION IN MORE THAN ONE IMPORTANT AREA OF THEIR LIVES. I, FOR EXAMPLE, CAN LIVE QUITE WELL WITH THE INSECURE INCOME OF A FREELANCER, WHILE I FIND IT DIFFICULT NOT TO SEE MY GIRLFRIEND FOR A LONG TIME AND NOT TO KNOW WHAT SHE IS DOING.

We live in a narcissistic society ~

Whatever you want to achieve in your life, you must patiently hold on to your dreams, take temporary setbacks into account and bear with long phases of uncertainty, my friend.

This is not easy in our narcissistic society. We are surrounded by people who want the "perfect partner", the "perfect job" or the "perfect house", now, but without being prepared to do their part of the hard emotional work that necessarily comes with such long-term and time-consuming projects.

The secret of your success: patience ~

As an adult you should be very careful to act out your wishes and fears immediately. Our desire to avoid uncertainty and always resolve everything at once is usually extremely damaging, both for us as well as for others, given the natural complexity and long history of most of our relationships.

Instead, you must be patient, bear with insecurity, fear and anger for minutes, hours and sometimes days, courageously accept the resulting pain and take your time to solve problems.

Are you willing to take full responsibility for your life, try to be more patient and bear with more uncertainty in the future?

Your patience will make a huge difference in your future relationships with other people—at work, in your family and with your partner—and it will also advance you in the art of presentation because you will become better in coping with fears, hard questions and unexpected incidents on stage.

"THE FIRST PRINCIPLE IS THE RECOGNITION OF OUR SHARED HUMANITY AND OUR SHARED ASPIRATION TO HAPPINESS AND THE AVOIDANCE OF SUFFERING: THE SECOND IS THE UNDERSTANDING OF INTERDEPENDENCE AS A KEY FEATURE OF HUMAN REALITY. FROM THESE TWO PRINCIPLES ... WE CAN DEVELOP A GENUINE CONCERN FOR OTHER'S WELL-BEING."

~ THE DALAI LAMA

ARE WE REALLY RESPONSIBLE FOR WHAT IS GOING ON ELSEWHERE, FAR AWAY FROM THE CITY IN WHICH WE LIVE?

SHOULD WE REALLY BE WORRYING ABOUT WHAT IS HAPPENING ON ANOTHER CONTINENT WITH PEOPLE WE HAVE NEVER MET AND WILL PROBABLY NEVER MEET, WITH WOMEN AND MEN WHO ARE NEITHER OUR SIBLINGS, NEPHEWS, COUSINS NOR OUR FRIENDS OR ACQUAINTANCES?

OUR BRAIN IS STILL VERY YOUNG ~

PERHAPS THE HISTORY OF OUR BRAIN CAN GIVE US AN ANSWER TO THIS QUESTION WHICH MANY OF US ARE CONCERNED ABOUT, TIME AND AGAIN.

TODAY, OUR BRAIN ABSORBS ABOUT 20% OF OUR TOTAL LIFE ENERGY, ROUND AROUND THE CLOCK, AND IT IS LARGER IN RELATION TO OUR BODY THAN THE BRAINS OF ALL OTHER ANIMALS ON THIS PLANET.

BUT OUR BRAIN WASN'T ALWAYS THIS BIG, IT HARDLY CHANGED IN HUNDREDS OF THOUSANDS OF YEARS UNTIL IT LITERALLY "EXPLODED" HALF A MILLION YEARS AGO. WHY? BECAUSE AT THIS POINT IN OUR HISTORY OUR ANCESTORS COMMITTED TO LIVING IN LARGER COMMUNITIES.

SUDDENLY, WE HAD TO MANAGE MUCH MORE RELATIONSHIPS WITH OTHER HUMANS THAN BEFORE, AND CONFRONTED WITH THIS NEW AND SOMETIMES LIFE-THREATENING COMPLEXITY, OUR BRAIN COULD ONLY DO ONE THING: BECOME LARGER AND MORE COMPLEX ITSELF.

WE ARE PROGRAMMED TO FEEL AND ACT LOCALLY ~

To return to the question we asked at the beginning: We can assume that our brain has grown to manage the direct relationships within our own community. If we look at the few tribes on this planet that still live like our ancestors, such as the Papua in Papua New Guinea, we see that the people there actually feel responsible only for a limited number of their fellow human beings.

The emotions that we regularly find in these tribes are love and care for their own family, their own friends and the members of their own tribe, and fear and distrust of individuals and groups that are not related, friends or allies to them.

Why? Because whenever several tribes of our ancestors lived as neighbours on the same territory, every crop failure forced them to compete with each other for the food they needed to survive. In such times, the advantages of war against one's neighbours often outweighed the advantages that had previously resulted from cooperation. Checking on the other tribes with a watchful eye, and to encounter strangers with suspicion until one could learn more about their intentions, was therefore an absolutely appropriate emotional behaviour at that time.

OUR FEELINGS ARE NO LONGER UP TO DATE ~

The problem with these "antique feelings" is that today, half a million years later, they no longer correspond to our living conditions.

Today, the most powerful tribes in the world can destroy not only the tribes directly competing with them, but also our planet as a whole together with their opponents.

In addition, in our modern, densely populated and economically interdependent world, the actions of each tribe always influence the life conditions of every other tribe. In fact, today the most pressing problems of any community—global warming, inequality and poverty—are also the problems of all

OTHER PEOPLE IN THE WORLD, PROBLEMS THAT ARE GLOBALLY INTERRELATED AND CAN THEREFORE ONLY BE SOLVED THROUGH COOPERATION ACROSS THE BORDERS—BEYOND THE LEGAL SYSTEMS OF INDIVIDUAL NATION STATES.

TODAY, FEELINGS SUCH AS FEAR OF STRANGERS, MISTRUST AND AGGRESSION ARE NO LONGER ABLE TO SECURE OUR SURVIVAL, ON THE CONTRARY, THEY ARE BOUND TO SEAL THE DOWNFALL OF HUMANITY AS A WHOLE.

WE MUST LEARN TO FEEL AND ACT GLOBALLY ~

WILL WE AS A HUMAN SPECIES BE ABLE TO REPROGRAM OUR BRAINS, OVERCOME OUR FEARS, OUR MISTRUST AND OUR AGGRESSIVE IMPULSES, AND ADVANCE TO A NEW DEFINITION OF WHO DOES BELONG TO OUR TRIBE?

WILL WE EVER BE ABLE TO WORK WITH PEOPLE OVER THE INTERNET AND SOLVE PROBLEMS WITH THEM, JUST AS WE ARE USED TO DO WITH GOOD FRIENDS AND ACQUAINTANCES, EVEN THOUGH THEY SPEAK A DIFFERENT LANGUAGE, BELIEVE IN ANOTHER GOD AND LIVE DIFFERENTLY THAN WE DO?

WILL WE ONE DAY REALISE THAT THE TRAGIC DEATH OF A LITTLE BOY OR GIRL IN A REFUGEE CAMP TEN THOUSAND MILES AWAY FROM OUR HOME MIGHT HAZARD OUR FIGHT AGAINST CANCER, UNEMPLOYMENT AND ENVIRONMENTAL DEGRADATION BECAUSE THAT CHILD WILL NEVER BECOME THE GREAT SCIENTIST, THE GIFTED POLITICIAN OR THE CREATIVE INVENTOR HE OR SHE COULD HAVE BEEN?

I BELIEVE THAT THE ANSWER TO THESE QUESTIONS IS "YES!". IT MAY TAKE CENTURIES, BUT IF AT SOME POINT WE WILL HAVE SUCCEEDED IN RAISING OUR SOULS, MINDS, BODIES AND HEARTS TO A FEELING OF CARE THAT SPANS THE WHOLE PLANET, WE WILL ALL FINALLY LIVE TOGETHER AS BROTHERS AND SISTERS.

WHENEVER YOU GO ON STAGE, PRETEND THIS DAY HAS ALREADY COME.

Buddha's Karaniya Metta Sutta—living with loving care:

I want to become skilled in doing good.
I want to experience that beautiful state of
lasting calm and harmony.
Therefore, from now on:

I will go on stage
and dedicate myself to my presentation
and stand perfectly upright in the truth.

I promise that I'll always remember
that there is only one thing really worth
wishing for:

That all living beings may be happy
and may feel safe,
and that they may enjoy lasting happiness
in their beautiful hearts.

And therefore:

I will not deceive anybody today,
I will not despise anyone, anywhere,
in anger or ill will,
and I will not wish anybody harm.

Just as I would guard my only child,
at the risk of my own life,
will I towards all beings
act with boundless kindness and a tender mind.

Today, my thoughts of boundless love
will shine bright and embrace the whole world,
above, below and in every direction there is,
without any imaginary boundaries,
without any hatred, or ill will or impatience.

"I know you're tired, but come, this is the way."

~ Rumi

Whenever I look back on my childhood, I think there was something that made me different from the other children I knew. At that time I had no word for it, but I still remember well that I often felt terribly alone, like the bearer of a dark secret who cannot share it with anyone.

This secret was that I could see and feel the grief and pain around me, that I could see and feel the despair and illusions of the adults around me, that I could see and feel how hard it was for everyone to get through life.

Today, I know the word for what I experienced so early: mindfulness. I was very early aware of the tragic half of human existence because I grew up without a father and in a family with very little love.

Accordingly, as a child I rarely experienced the other half of our existence which consists of trust, ease and joy.

Probably, that's why I started looking for the underlying patterns of quarrelling, loneliness and misfortune instead of going to birthday parties or riding ponies. Over time, I became good at understanding our human situation, but the disappointing and hurtful thing was that I did become more and more sad by doing so.

Understanding needs more than the mind ~

My growing understanding of the psychological, economic and political context of the human condition did make me sad because I realised that the whole history of humanity—and not only my personal experience—was to a large extent a story of bleak, ongoing despair.

In fact, it took me many years of depression to realise a fundamental truth about myself and the world in which we all live: understanding life with the mind alone never leads to a positive transformation of our reality, the progress of our mind must always be accompanied by the growth of our heart.

Essentially, we must learn to say "Yes!" to existence with all its brutal aspects with our whole heart, while our mind goes on saying relentlessly "No!, no!, no!".

Ideas alone change nothing ~

I know that I risk to lose you at this point. No doubt, it is not easy to understand that we must accept war, hunger and slavery emotionally in order to make the world a better place for all of us.

But without acceptance in our hearts, we will reject reality—and the people as they are today—and seek to escape the now, and consequently we will miss the only chance to change our lives and this world: to go beyond despair over the world as it is, and to do what's possible to change it to the better for the benefit of all of us.

This is, by the way, one of the many insights that the art of presentation bestows on us: again and again I see people coming on stage who lack the willingness to connect with the real audience in the room instead of talking to the imaginary audience in their heads.

They think that their ideas will change the world, that it's enough to be right, even if nobody in the room connects with them.

But if we do not reach the hearts of the people around us, we cannot get them to join the great wave of transformation. We must go beyond the fear of the world and the people as they are today and seek communion with them, for healing does not happen mainly in our heads but in our hearts.

By accepting the unacceptable, we heal ~

You and I, we can and will fight together to end war and inequality and the dictatorship of the Few over the Many, but part of our existence will always remain tragic—and part of the people around us will always walk back and forth along the banks of the river without finding the bridge to the other side, as Buddha once so beautifully put it.

This cannot be otherwise, for the duality of our existence creates different levels of awareness, growth and enlightenment which must all coexist at the same point in time.

By accepting what is actually unacceptable with our hearts, we merge for a moment and for another and for another with the great spirit, with the great totality, with the great unifying love that reigns the universe. And suddenly, and beyond any logic, everything is good.

"Learn to observe your emotions without needing to act or distract yourself from them. Within that stillness your truest, most vulnerable thoughts will arise, and it is these thoughts that will show you where your healing work must begin."

~ Alaric Hutchinson

We are all drug addicts, and we all share the same addiction: action.

Things and people around us must not come to a standstill, and we must not lose contact with them for a moment, because we need new challenges and surprises, news and offers every second—so that we do not have to feel the emptiness within ourselves.

The carousel has to turn without ever pausing, day and night, until we are finally so tired that we can switch off and forget ourselves—in front of the TV, in front of a bottle of wine, by finally going to sleep. But somewhere between one turn of this carousel and the next, something gets lost: our inner silence.

Most of us cannot tell this inner silence from boredom. Did you read about the experiment where the participants had to wait half an hour in a room without distractions? The only thing they were offered, in order to avoid boredom, was the possibility of giving themselves electroshocks—which most participants actually did. Because even that seemed better to them than not being able to do anything at all.

Everything will fall into place ~

But it is precisely this inaction that we must face if we want to grow as human beings. We must listen to ourselves again and again with patience and learn to welcome our sadness, our loneliness and our fragility whenever they come to the surface of our consciousness.

By taking note of our supposedly negative emotions and slowly clearing them up—instead of constantly avoiding them—we learn to integrate them and use them to our benefit. The English language has a beautiful expression for this, "Things will fall into place."

We will get back an incredible amount of life energy if we manage to bear with our painful emotions, thus clearing them and letting them find their adequate place.

I would be lying if I said that this is the only reasonable strategy to deal with painful experiences and feelings. Not confronting our negative emotions, especially shortly after a traumatic event, can sometimes be the better option.

But my own depression has shown me that sooner or later we have to become aware of our inner pain if we do not want to lose a big part of our life energy and with it both our mental and physical health.

All pain that is repressed and not confronted and worked with, binds energy, and this blocked energy does not disappear: it stays in our body, searching for other ways to eventually make it to the surface of our consciousness.

Thus, what we started in order not to feel bad, might end in mental and physical illness and even worse experiences for ourselves.

Cleared negativity is the basis ~

In confronting us with mental and physical problems, our subconscious repeats the process that our universe uses to stimulate us to grow: life first breaks us up, then we rebuild ourselves with more awareness, this awareness then begins to heal ourselves and others, and consequently we grow, until —life breaks us up again.

The universe loves us in a wild fashion, and it will therefore always force us into situations bound to bring our repressed energies to the surface.

The power struggle in the workplace, the breaking up of a relationship, the conflict with a friend: a lot of this happens—also—to help us to confront our suppressed feelings, to clear them and thus become able to experience more love.

Our universe does everything out of love, and every hurtful event in this universe creates—in the long run—a level of existence that contains more love than the one before. To transcend pain into love is therefore the master path to a life in synchronicity with the universe and its eternal laws.

By practicing inner silence, we lay the foundation for that powerful, authentic and emotionally rich life the universe wants us to live—and for those powerful, authentic and emotionally rich presentations the universe wants us to deliver.

ENSURE EQUALITY:

Women must have the same opportunities to get involved in society, in business & in politics & make their dreams come true as men—anywhere & anytime.

Make sure that the women & men in your organisation, your company & your family are equally challenged & equally supported in mastering those challenges.

The language you use during your presentations is very important in this respect because our words not only reflect reality, they also can change and transform it. Therefore, whenever you are on stage & give examples, you should use "she" and "he", & you should always show faces, quotes and results of and by men & women alike.

One last thing: equality does not mean equal treatment. Giving a fish, a lizard, & a monkey the same chance to climb a tree is not providing them with equal opportunities.

In my experience, women regularly use longer sentences, thematise more aspects & alternatives & often speak with a slightly higher voice.

Equality does not mean that women have the opportunity to present like men, it means that they have the opportunity to present as they see fit without fearing disadvantages for their careers.

"THERE IS NO WISHING WITHOUT TRANSCENDENCY, AND THERE IS NO HOPING WITHOUT THE LONGING TO ESCAPE THE LIMITING HORIZONS OF MY 'I'. THE MORE I RELATE MYSELF TO OTHERS, THE MORE I GET TRANSFORMED."

~ EUGENIO BORGNA

WHY IS IT SO IMPORTANT FOR US TO DEVELOP OUR ABILITY TO LOVE? BECAUSE IT HELPS US AVOID THE ONLY SIN THAT EXISTS: INDIFFERENCE—TO OURSELVES, TO OTHER PEOPLE AND TO LIFE AS A WHOLE.

INDIFFERENCE IS OUR REACTION TO ALIENATION, DISAPPOINTMENT AND THE FEELING OF NOT BEING LOVED. GIVING IN TO INDIFFERENCE MEANS SUPPRESSING OUR INNATE LONGING FOR LOVE IN ORDER TO AVOID REJECTION, DISAPPOINTMENT AND BITTERNESS. INDIFFERENCE ULTIMATELY MEANS CHOOSING DEATH OVER LIFE, SO THAT WE NO LONGER HAVE TO SUFFER.

BEING ABLE TO LOVE, ON THE OTHER HAND, MEANS LETTING OTHERS TOGETHER WITH THEIR FEELINGS AND IDEAS INTO OUR LIFE, WITH ALL THE PAIN, DISAPPOINTMENTS AND TEARS THAT MAY COME ALONG WITH IT. IT MEANS TO LEAVE THE WEAPON-STARING TOWER OF LONELINESS AND DIVE HEADFIRST INTO THE MIGHTY BUT ULTIMATELY LOVING WAVES OF LIFE.

GO ON STAGE AND EMBRACE LIFE ~

AS LONG AS WE BLAME LIFE AS IT IS, THE PEOPLE AS THEY ARE AND OURSELVES AS WE ARE, FOR THE PAIN THAT COMES WITH IT, WE ARE NOT READY FOR THE STAGE AND THE ART OF PRESENTATION. UNLESS WE ACCEPT OURSELVES, OTHERS AND LIFE AS A WHOLE, OUR PRESENTATIONS WILL NOT BE AN INSTRUMENT OF HOPE.

EVERY AUDIENCE ON THIS EARTH CAN FEEL IN A SECOND WHETHER YOU COME ON STAGE AS A BITTER HERMIT OR AS A BENEVOLENT AMBASSADOR OF HUMANITY, WHETHER YOU ARE REALLY READY TO CONNECT WITH OTHER PEOPLE OR NOT.

If you have not overcome the feeling of separation and the resulting indifference within yourself, you are not yet ready to give people hope—no matter how wise and well-prepared you might be.

EVERY EMBRACE ON STAGE IS A PROMISE ~

Imagine a man or a woman on stage, imagine his face, her face. You can see him thinking, you can see that she is somewhere else, caught in the labyrinth of language and abstract ideas, in the middle of which the temples of lifeless science and loveless history reign over everything else.

And now imagine how she suddenly spreads her arms, how he suddenly looks at you and symbolically accepts and embraces you and the whole audience.

Magic.

Our ideas are undoubtedly important, facts and figures can help us test our visions against reality and history can teach us many things: but not without a hug, not without connecting with other people, not without hope.

What every audience in the world really wants is communion. We all want to reach, at least for a few moments, that magical state in which our "I" merges with that of others to a magical, ecstatic "We", thus revealing all the possibilities open to us.

Ultimately, our lives are not about exchanging and owning information, ideas or products, but about going beyond our disappointment, our loneliness and our indifference.

Ultimately, every life is about seeing our existence as difficult as it really is and yet trying to live with hope gleaming in our hearts.

Ultimately, life is a course in learning to love.

TIP ~

BECOME AWARE OF YOUR PERSONAL BASELINE:

~ HOW DO YOU SEE YOURSELF?
"I AM ..."

~ HOW DO YOU SEE THE OTHER PEOPLE?
"THEY ARE ..."

~ HOW DO YOU SEE THE WORLD AS A WHOLE?
"THE WORLD IS ..."

SO, HOW'S YOUR PERSONAL "BASELINE"? IS IT LIFE-AFFIRMING OR AN EXPRESSION OF YOUR INNER DESPAIR, DOES IT GIVE YOU & OTHERS HOPE, OR IS IT MAKING EVERYBODY MORE DEPRESSED, DOES IT EXPRESS COMPASSION, OR IS IT A MANIFESTO OF INDIFFERENCE? WHATEVER IT IS, YOU CAN'T PRETEND TO BE SOMEONE ELSE ON STAGE.

THAT IS WHY YOU SHOULD ADAPT YOUR CURRENT PRESENTATION-STYLE TO YOUR CURRENT BASELINE.

IF YOU'RE SAD & WORRIED RIGHT NOW, START BY TALKING ABOUT YOUR FEARS & DOUBTS RATHER THAN TRYING TO BE A SELF-CONFIDENT SUPERHERO.

IF SOMETHING ANNOYS YOU RIGHT NOW, TELL YOUR AUDIENCE RIGHT AT THE BEGINNING WHAT IT IS INSTEAD OF PRETENDING TO BE ABOVE EVERYTHING.

IF YOU'RE HAPPY, SHARE YOUR JOY.

THE PEOPLE IN YOUR AUDIENCE WILL APPRECIATE YOUR HONESTY—AS LONG AS YOU LET THEM GO HOME WITH A FINAL HUG, A FINAL SMILE & A FINAL WORD OF HOPE.

"The more you understand, the more you love; the more you love, the more you understand. They are two sides of one reality."

~ Thich Nhat Hanh

"Samsara": everything around us is constantly changing, yes, but without really leading to a transformation and to a solution to our problems.

With each new technology new jobs are created, but old ones are destroyed, with each new scientific knowledge old questions are answered, but even more pressing ones raised, and when a famine, persecution or war finally end on one continent, the horror starts all over again somewhere else.

It feels like being in a room without time, on the walls the photographs of the dead Sioux displaced from their pastures, the young Sicilian immigrants freezing in the blizzard ridden streets of New York, the young girls standing at their machines in the toy factories in Shanghai.

It is always the same look, never really changing over the centuries, it's always the same pain, never being really healed, it's always the same "Why?", never really answered.

It's there on their faces, like a cry: samsara.

But we don't want to look at their faces, we are afraid of letting their pain into our hearts, afraid that their sorrow will submerge our souls with a tsunami of tears, overwhelming us.

You and I have learned to escape from this seemingly endless cycle of destruction, futile hope and ever new suffering by burying our true nature and our real needs under a mountain of substitute satisfaction—like worthless technical gadgets, unhealthy food and needy relationships.

WE NEED TO REDISCOVER OUR REAL NEEDS ~

In order to overcome Samsara, we must let go of all substitute satisfactions and become a "Sramana", a homeless wanderer amidst the shining skyscrapers of cheap hopes, false promises and abstract thoughts.

Our gypsy heart knows that our life goal must be transformation, not change.

In order to break the ever turning spokes of Samsara, we must gradually abandon the substitutes for consciousness, self-love and love and immerse ourselves in the underlying waves of compassion, goodness and enlightened action.

Only the rediscovery of our true nature and our real needs, both on the personal and global level, can transform us and bring us to a higher level of spirituality.

FOLLOW YOUR GYPSY HEART ~

If we succeed in substituting narcissism and selfishness through goodwill and love, ideology and false religion through truth and understanding, fossil energies through renewable energies, destructive materialism through essentialism, secret services through agencies for the people, private banks for the Few through banks for the Many, hidden power structures through transparent ones, individual transportation through meaningful commuter systems, tax evasion through just taxation and inequality through opportunities for everyone, the wheel of Samsara one fine day will finally stop turning.

Going on stage with this awareness today, will help to transform our world and bring that day about sooner.

TIP ~

THE EIGHTFOLD PATH LEADING TO YOUR ENLIGHTENMENT, ACCORDING TO BUDDHA:

WISDOM

The right view—Am I willing & able to see how things really are?

The right intention—Do I pursue only those goals that are really worthy of my soul?

VIRTUE

The right speech—How can I heal with my words instead of hurting other beings through them?

The right action—How can I act compassionately instead of harming other beings?

The right livelihood—How can I make a living virtuously & share the resulting wealth instead of exploiting other beings?

AWARENESS

The right effort—How can I deepen my good qualities while trying to integrate the harmful ones?

The right mindfulness—How can I become more conscious while trying to live in the now?

The right focus—How can I control my mind & emotions while trying to create peace, goodness & happiness within me.

The Eightfold Path to an enlightened presentation:

Wisdom

The right view—Am I honest with myself & the audience, have I considered all relevant facts?

The right intention—Is the message of my presentation clear & suited to encourage & strengthen my audience?

Virtue

The right speech—Is my dialogue with the audience based on respect, compassion & sincerity?

The right action—Is the goal of my presentation truly to make the world a better place?

The right livelihood—Is my organisation & its product, its service or its idea really good for the environment & the people?

Awareness

The right effort—Does my presentation show the real advantages & disadvantages & help to solve existing problems?

The right mindfulness—Does my presentation increase the perception of my audience on the spiritual, mental, emotional & physical level?

The right focus—Am I ready to be truly myself during my presentation, fully present & open for my audience?

"I STOOD BEFORE A SILKWORM ONE DAY, AND THAT NIGHT MY HEART SAID TO ME: 'YOU KNOW, I CAN DO THINGS LIKE THAT, I CAN SPIN SKIES, I CAN BE WOVEN INTO LOVE THAT CAN BRING WARMTH TO PEOPLE, I CAN BE SOFT AGAINST A CRYING FACE, I CAN BE WINGS THAT LIFT, AND I CAN TRAVEL ON MY THOUSAND FEET THROUGHOUT THE WORLD, MY SACS FILLED WITH THE SACRED.' AND I REPLIED TO MY HEART: 'DEAR, CAN YOU REALLY DO ALL THOSE THINGS?' AND IT JUST NODDED 'YES!' IN SILENCE. SO WE BEGAN AND WILL NEVER CEASE."

~ RUMI

WE SHOULD ALL STRIVE FIRST AND FOREMOST TO BECOME LOVERS, TO BECOME MASTERS IN THE ART OF LOVE. I'M NOT SURE LOVE IS REALLY ALL WE NEED, AS THE HEROES OF MY CHILDHOOD, THE BEATLES, ONCE SANG, BUT I'M SURE THAT THE AMOUNT OF LOVE WE WILL BE ABLE TO LIBERATE WITHIN US WILL EVENTUALLY MAKE THE DIFFERENCE IN OUR STRUGGLE FOR SURVIVAL AS HUMANITY.

WE ALL HAVE TO LEARN THE ART OF LOVE ~

IF I ASKED YOU HERE AND NOW TO PAINT AN OIL PAINTING FOR ME OR CARVE A SCULPTURE OUT OF A BLOCK OF MARBLE, WOULD YOU BE ABLE TO DO SO? YOU'RE SMILING. PROBABLY NOT, RIGHT? FOR PAINTING AND SCULPTURE ARE ARTS, AND WE BOTH KNOW PERFECTLY WELL THAT IT TAKES MANY YEARS OF LEARNING, DEVOTION AND PRACTICE TO FINALLY MASTER AN ART.

BUT WHY THEN ARE WE MADE TO BELIEVE FROM CHILDHOOD ON THAT WE ARE ALL CAPABLE OF LOVING AT ANY AGE, AT ANY TIME AND FOREVER?

THE ART OF LOVE IS NOT TAUGHT IN KINDERGARTEN, SCHOOL OR UNIVERSITY. WHY? NOT BECAUSE THIS WOULD NOT BE DESIRABLE, RIGHT? THE TRUTH IS THAT WE ALL LONG TO

GIVE LOVE AND EXPERIENCE LOVE, AND THAT WE WOULD THEREFORE BE WELL ADVISED TO LEARN HOW TO BUILD AND FOSTER DEEP AND LASTING LOVE RELATIONSHIPS AS EARLY AS POSSIBLE IN OUR LIVES.

NO, THE REASON FOR THIS UNREALISTIC APPROACH TO LOVE IN OUR SOCIETY IS THAT OUR ECONOMIC SYSTEM NEEDS CONSUMERS WHO ARE WILLING TO BUY THE THOUSAND PROMISING BUT LOVELESS PRODUCTS THAT ARE OFFERED TO US EVERY MINUTE AS A SUBSTITUTE FOR LOVE.

WILL YOU DIE WITHOUT HAVING LOVED? ~

THIS IS THE TRUE TRAGEDY OF OUR TIME, FROM WHICH ALL OTHER TRAGEDIES DERIVE: MOST OF US LIVE IN A STATE OF CONSTANT SELF-DOUBT, FRUSTRATION AND LONELINESS WITHOUT EVER HAVING LEARNED TO LOVE AND ACCEPT LOVE.

YES, I KNOW THAT SOUNDS EXAGGERATED, BUT I DO BELIEVE THAT ALMOST ALL OF US ARE IN GREAT DANGER OF DYING WITHOUT EVER HAVING TASTED THE ALL-TRANSFORMING ELIXIR OF HIGHER LOVE.

DO YOU REALLY WANT TO BELONG TO THOSE WHO NEVER EXPERIENCE REAL LOVE AND ARE NEVER BORN AS TRUE HUMAN BEINGS BEFORE THEY DIE?

IF YOU WANT TO AVOID THIS SAD FATE, YOU MUST MAKE LOVE THE MAIN GOAL IN YOUR LIFE AND DEVOTE MUCH OF YOUR TIME TO THE PURSUE OF LOVE. YOU WILL THEN HAVE TO LEARN TO GO BEYOND "EROS", THE SENSUAL, PASSIONATE DESIRE, AND TO MERGE IT WITH "AGAPE", THE SPIRITUAL LOVE, AND YOU WILL ALSO HAVE TO MAKE SURE THAT IN TIME YOU MAKE "PHILIA", YOUR LOVE FOR YOUR FAMILY AND FRIENDS, THE BASIS FOR "AI", THE UNIVERSAL LOVE FOR EVERY LIVING BEING.

SO, I ASK YOU AGAIN, ARE YOU READY TO DEVOTE YOUR LIFE TO THE ART OF LOVING?

GOOD, BECAUSE YOUR NEXT PRESENTATION WILL BE A GREAT OPPORTUNITY TO PRACTICE THE ART OF LOVE.

REMEMBER YOUR BASELINE, "I AM...", "THEY ARE ..." AND "THE WORLD IS ..."? TRY TO FINISH THESE SENTENCES IN A WAY THAT THEY BECOME A PROGRAM FOR MORE LOVE BEFORE YOU ARE GOING ON STAGE THE NEXT TIME.

"AS YOUR RESPECT FOR YOURSELF GROWS BECAUSE OF THE COURAGE YOU DEMONSTRATE IN FACING YOURSELF, YOUR RESPECT FOR OTHERS WILL ALSO GROW BECAUSE THIS IS AN EXTENSION OF YOUR RESPECT FOR YOURSELF. SO TOO, AS YOUR SELF LOVE GROWS, YOUR LOVE FOR OTHERS—REAL LOVE—WILL COME INTO EXISTENCE."

~ JOHN RUSKAN

How is it possible that a person we didn't even know to exist a minute ago can suddenly become the centre of our thoughts, feelings and dreams? To me, this is one of the greatest miracles of our lives.

As soon as this miracle has happened, we are overwhelmed by sweet anticipation. This woman or this man, partly still a stranger, partly strangely familiar, becomes the promise of ecstasy, joy and perfection with every look, gesture and movement she or he bestows on us, promises us godlike wholeness as well as very human pleasure.

LOVE BLINDS US TO MAKE US SEE BETTER ~

It would be completely wrong to assume that this anticipation of perfection is just a trick of nature to lead us together and therefore an illusion. Love, on the contrary, paints in our hearts a very realistic picture of what could be whenever two people fall in love with each other. Love, being the eternal law reigning over all the universes there are, never lies, it always shows us a possible future.

However, on the way to that future, we have to clear a lot of repressed hurt, rage and fear. That is why we have chosen this one person in a million, to be happy in the long run, yes, but also in order to experience our being broken in the short run as the precondition for growing towards love. With the loving support of the universe, we have unconsciously

BUT WITH THE PRECISION OF A SLEEPWALKER FOUND EXACTLY THE PERSON WHO CAN AND WILL FREE FIRST THE PAIN AND THEN THE LOVE HIDDEN WITHIN US.

THEREFORE, AS SOON AS YOU TWO FALL IN LOVE, YOU SHOULD PREPARE EQUALLY FOR THE MOST BEAUTIFUL AS WELL AS FOR THE MOST DIFFICULT HOURS OF YOUR LIFE BECAUSE SOON SHE OR HE WILL BEHAVE IN SUCH A WAY THAT YOU WILL FEEL HURT, BETRAYED AND DECEIVED BETWEEN ONE PERFECT MOMENT AND THE NEXT.

AND THAT IS EXACTLY WHAT LIFE WANTED TO ACHIEVE WITH THIS LOVE RELATIONSHIP FROM THE BEGINNING: TO MAKE YOUR REPRESSED HURT COME TO THE SURFACE WITH THE HELP OF A LOVING PERSON, IN ORDER TO CLEAR THIS PAIN AND ADVANCE TOWARDS DEEP, REAL, TIMELESS LOVE.

YOU ARE NOT A LOVER—NOT YET ~

NEVER FORGET: THAT YOU ARE ABLE TO FALL IN LOVE AND ACTUALLY DO FALL IN LOVE DOES NOT MEAN THAT YOU ARE A LOVER, OR THAT YOU KNOW WHAT LOVE REALLY IS. FALLING IN LOVE GIFTS YOU WITH A GLIMPSE OF REAL LOVE, NOT MORE AND NOT LESS THAN THAT.

WHAT YOU PERCEIVE AS LOVE AT THE MOMENT IS VERY PROBABLY IN LARGE PART MUTUAL NEED AND USE, AND NOT THE HIGHER LOVE YOU ARE PREDETERMINED TO.

DOES YOUR LIFE FEEL MEANINGLESS WITHOUT YOUR PARTNER, DO YOU EXPERIENCE A FEELING OF EMPTINESS WHEN SHE OR HE IS NOT AROUND, DO YOU FEEL INSECURE AND OUT OF LOVE WHEN HE OR SHE DOES NOT GIVE YOU WHAT YOU NEED RIGHT NOW?

THAT'S THE OPPOSITE OF LOVE, FRAMED IN GLIMPSES OF REAL LOVE, AND IF YOU DON'T EXERCISE GREAT CARE, YOU SOON WILL FEEL THE URGE TO CONTROL HER AND RESTRICT HIM, TO YELL AT HIM OR THREATEN HER, TO TAKE REVENGE ON HER OR JUST LEAVE HIM.

DOES ALL THIS SOUND FAMILIAR? ASK YOURSELF WITH AN OPEN HEART: WOULD A TRUE LOVER, WOULD A MASTER IN THE ART OF LOVE, DO ALL THIS?

NO, LIKE I SAID, RIGHT NOW YOU ONLY DO BELIEVE THAT YOU HAVE UNDERSTOOD THE ESSENCE OF LOVE, BUT YOU ARE

NOT REALLY WITH YOURSELF AND NOT REALLY WITH YOUR PARTNER, YOU ARE NOT REALLY LISTENING TO YOURSELF, AND YOU ARE NOT REALLY LISTENING TO YOUR PARTNER, YOU DO NOT REALLY UNDERSTAND WHY YOU REACT THE WAY YOU DO, AND WHY YOUR PARTNER DOES. NOT YET.

NOW IMAGINE WHAT YOUR LIFE WILL LOOK LIKE WHEN ONE DAY YOU WILL HAVE BECOME A TRUE MASTER OF LOVE, AND WHAT IT WILL FEEL LIKE TO GO ON STAGE, THEN.

IMAGINE HOW EASY YOU WILL FEEL WITHOUT THAT HEAVY DOUBT IN YOU WHETHER YOU ARE WORTHY OF AND ABLE TO LOVE.

IMAGINE THAT FEELING OF FREEDOM AND SECURITY IN YOU AS YOU SHARE YOUR INNER RICHNESS WITH YOUR AUDIENCE AS WELL AS YOUR JOY AT THE FACT THAT YOU CAN BOTH GIVE AND RECEIVE LOVE, NOW—WITHOUT CLINGING, WITHOUT FEAR OF LOSS AND WITHOUT NEEDING AND USING EACH OTHER.

IMAGINE THAT.

TIP ~

BELIEVE IN THE POWER OF YOUR PRAYERS:

WHETHER YOU BELIEVE IN THE EXISTENCE OF A DIVINE BEING OR NOT, WHETHER YOU ARE INSPIRED BY ONE OF THE KNOWN RELIGIONS OR NOT: PRAY!

PRAY FOR YOURSELF, FOR THOSE YOU LOVE & ALSO FOR THOSE YOU HAVE NEVER MET & MAY NEVER MEET IN YOUR LIFE.

YOUR PRAYER IS A WAY TO LET GOODNESS GROW IN YOURSELF, TO RADIATE IT &, FINALLY, TO LET IT REACH BEYOND TIME & SPACE.

I MYSELF HAVE ALWAYS FOUND THE BUDDHIST SCRIPTURE "PATISAMBHIDAMAGGA" INSPIRING, AN ANCIENT PRAYER TRADITIONALLY ATTRIBUTED TO BUDDHA'S DISCIPLE SARIPUTTA. IT CONTAINS THIS BEAUTIFUL LINE:

"MAY ALL BEINGS LIVE FREE FROM DANGER, DISTRESS & FEAR & EXPERIENCE TRUE & LASTING HAPPINESS."

YOU CAN USE THESE SIMPLE WORDS TO START TO RADIATE GOODNESS WHENEVER YOU COMMENCE TO PRAY—OR WHATEVER YOU LIKE TO CALL IT:

BEGIN WITH THE WORDS: "MAY I MYSELF BE FREE FROM ...".

THEN YOU CAN THINK OF SOMEONE YOU LOVE: "MAY ... BE FREE FROM ...".

THEN YOU CAN CONNECT WITH SOMEONE WITH WHOM YOU HAVE A DIFFICULT RELATIONSHIP WITH: "MAY ALSO ... BE FREE FROM ...".

THEN YOU CAN PRAY FOR SOMEONE WHO YOU CONSIDER A BAD PERSON: "MAY ... BE FREE FROM ... AND LIVE HAPPILY EVER AFTER."

FINALLY, YOU SHOULD INCLUDE ALL THE PEOPLE ON THIS PLANET IN YOUR PRAYER, ALL BEINGS IN OUR & EVERY OTHER UNIVERSE & FINALLY ALL BEINGS WHO HAVE EVER LIVED & WILL EVER LIVE.

"THE MOST PRECIOUS INHERITANCE THAT PARENTS CAN GIVE THEIR CHILDREN IS THEIR OWN HAPPINESS."

~ THICH NHAT THANH

IMAGINE YOU WERE GOING ON STAGE, FACING A FEW HUNDRED PEOPLE WHO DIDN'T KNOW YOU, AND STARTING YOUR PRESENTATION LIKE THIS:

"PLEASE LET ME SAY SOMETHING IMPORTANT TO ME BEFORE THE ACTUAL START OF MY PRESENTATION: I'M GLAD THAT I'M ALIVE RIGHT NOW, AND I'M GLAD THAT YOU ARE ALIVE RIGHT NOW. IN THIS MOMENT, I AM FEELING LOVE FOR MYSELF, AND ALTHOUGH I DON'T REALLY KNOW YOU, SYMPATHY FOR ALL OF YOU. WHY? BECAUSE YOU ARE HERE TODAY, WITH ME, ACCOMPANYING ME ON THIS INCREDIBLE JOURNEY THROUGH SPACE AND TIME, ON THIS FRAGILE SPACESHIP CALLED EARTH, AND WE ARE ALL TOGETHER IN THIS."

WOULD YOU EVER START YOUR PRESENTATION LIKE THAT?

JUST BETWEEN ME AND YOU, I MYSELF HAVE PRESENTED AND SPOKEN TO STRANGERS HUNDREDS OF TIMES AND NEVER INTRODUCED A PRESENTATION WITH THESE WORDS. BUT ONCE IN A WHILE I FELT LIKE THIS WHILE BEING ON STAGE.

NOW, WOULDN'T IT BE GREAT IF WE COULD FEEL LIKE THAT EVERY TIME WE GO ON STAGE, AND, EVEN BETTER, IF WE COULD FEEL THIS WAY ALL THROUGH OUR LIFETIME?

SELF-LOVE HAPPENS ONLY IN THE NOW ~

UNFORTUNATELY, THE REALITY IS QUITE DIFFERENT: WE ALL LIVE ONLY A FEW DAYS OF THE YEAR WITH A WARM FEELING OF LOVE IN OUR HEARTS, OR SO IT LOOKS TO ME. WHY IS THAT SO? BECAUSE WE LINGER MUCH TOO OFTEN IN THE MIND, AND OUR MINDS CONSTANTLY WANDER BACK AND FORTH BETWEEN THE PAST, THE PRESENT AND THE FUTURE. IN THIS WAY, HOWEVER, WE POSTPONE SELF-ACCEPTANCE AND SELF-LOVE, THE PRECONDITION FOR LOVING OTHERS, OVER AND OVER AGAIN:

~ "One day, I'll weigh ten pounds less, look in the mirror and like myself."

~ "One day, I'll find the right partner and feel loved."

~ "One day, I'll get the recognition I crave and finally be happy."

It is not wrong per se to work on your body and to strive for love and recognition, but are you sure that in the future it will really be easier to accept and love yourself than today?

I think we all must try to love more, today, here and now, no matter how much we weigh, no matter whether we live in a relationship or not and no matter how much recognition is given to us right now.

Self-love and love are not only the ultimate goal of human development, they are, at the same time, also the starting point and turning point of human development because they are, even if unconsciously, already there in our body, just waiting to be felt by us. Felt, not thought.

Imagine a World Full of Self-Love and Love ~

I firmly believe that the path to the liberation of humanity leads through our body and our ability to feel regularly self-love and love on the physical level. Meditation, breathing exercises, yoga, autogenic training and Jacobson's muscle-relaxation-technique are not only ways to live more in the now and to awaken the self-love and love dormant in our body: they also will change the world as a whole.

Imagine a presentation in which everything that is said and shown, is said and shown out of a feeling of awakened kindness. Imagine a world in which gratitude, love and the wish for the well-being of all living beings are no longer just pious wishes for a distant future, but are lived and experienced in the present.

Can you imagine what such a world would feel like?

MY SYMBOL OF UNIVERSAL LOVE. CUT IT OUT, AND SEND YOUR GOOD WISHES OUT INTO THE UNIVERSE.

OUTLOOK ~
WHO WE WANT TO BE

"EVIL IS A SOURCE OF MORAL INTELLIGENCE IN THE SENSE THAT WE NEED TO LEARN FROM OUR SHADOW, FROM OUR DARK SIDE, IN ORDER TO BE GOOD."

~ JOHN BRADSHAW

WHO IS RESPONSIBLE FOR HAVING MADE OUR WORLD THE WAY IT IS? WELL, I GUESS IT'S YOU AND I. I KNOW WHAT YOU ARE GOING TO SAY NOW: "WAIT, THE FEW BEHIND THE PRESIDENTS AND PRIME MINISTERS HAVE THE POWER, NOT US, THE MANY, RIGHT? SO, IT'S THEM WHO ARE RESPONSIBLE."

RIGHT, BUT THIS ENORMOUS POWER OF THE FEW DOESN'T ACTUALLY COME FROM THEIR MONEY, THEIR THINK TANKS AND THEIR HIRED HIT MEN. THEIR REAL POWER COMES FROM THE FACT THAT WE ARE ALL THEIR ACCOMPLICES.

WE ARE IN IT WITH THEM ~

YOU AND I, WE KNOW FROM THE BOTTOM OF OUR HEARTS THAT WHENEVER THE FEW ATTACK AND EXPROPRIATE THE NEXT NATION, WE ARE PART OF IT. AND SO DO THE FEW. THEY KNOW THAT WE KNOW THAT OUR SECOND CAR AND OUR SECOND COMPUTER—THAT WHAT WE CALL OUR "WEALTH"—IS BASED ON THE POVERTY OF THE EXPLOITED 16-YEAR-OLD GIRLS IN THE TOY FACTORIES, SMARTPHONE BARRACKS AND T-SHIRT SHELTERS IN CHINA, MALAYSIA AND BANGLADESH.

THEY KNOW THAT YOU AND I ALLOWED THEM TO KILL JOHN F. KENNEDY, OLAF PALME AND ALFRED HERRHAUSEN, THAT YOU AND I ALLOWED THEM TO ATTACK AFGHANISTAN, IRAQ AND SYRIA, THAT YOU AND I ALLOWED THEM TO STAGE FALSE TERRORIST ATTACKS ALL OVER THE WORLD IN TOTAL PEACE.

THE FEW KNOW THAT THE ANCIENT BEAST THAT THEY ARE WORSHIPPING IS SLUMBERING ALSO IN YOU AND ME: SATAN, THE DEVIL, DIABLO, DJINN, DYBBUK—THE DARK, ANGRY, GREEDY CREATURE WHO WANTS TO WHIP, RAPE AND SET FIRE, AND REJOICES BEHIND OUR MASK OF RESERVE AND KINDNESS WHILE THE FEW LAY THE WORLD IN RUINS.

As above, so below, as inside, so outside ~

Although I firmly believe that we were all born with a natural tendency towards kindness and love, I am also convinced that this goodwill is in constant struggle with the destructive emotions and impulses that we also carry within us.

Our computers, satellites and robots won't be able to help us in this fight, my friend. Our technology is not neutral, it serves above all to make us more and more productive and controllable.

"And what about science?", you ask? I have spent 30 years of my life at universities all over the world, believe me when I say that they are largely financed by the Few and accordingly work on the consolidation of our bondage and not on our liberation.

We, you and I, have to do the job ourselves, we have to face our own shadows and learn to transform fear, greed and destructive rage to free ourselves from the bloody shackles that bind us to the murderous Few.

Begin the greatest transformation of all ~

Every transformation of our reality begins with our own transformation, begins with a courageous decision: not to wait any longer and to start a new life today, in the here and now, a new life that will use the energy and passion of our dark demons to make ourselves and the world brighter.

Without this transformation within us, every revolution on the outside is doomed to fail. Without it, every attempt to turn this world into a garden of Eden will end in barbed wire and blood sprained prison walls.

The greatest and most important struggle in the history of mankind is taking place right now. Within yourself.

What are you going to do?

TIP ~

YOUR TEN STEPS ON THE WAY TO A NEW LIFE:

~ START BY GETTING TO KNOW YOURSELF BETTER. LOOK AT YOURSELF, FEEL YOURSELF, THINK ABOUT YOURSELF. BECOME AWARE OF WHO YOU REALLY ARE & BECOME AWARE OF WHO YOU ARE NOT.

~ LEARN TO ENDURE SUFFERING. NOT EVERY PLEASANT CONDITION IS BENEFICIAL TO US, & NOT EVERY UNPLEASANT CONDITION IS HARMFUL.

~ LEARN TO CONTROL YOUR DESTRUCTIVE IMPULSES, ACCEPT THEM, BUT DO NOT ACT UNDER THEIR INFLUENCE. LEAVE THE SCENE OF AN ARGUMENT, SLEEP ONE NIGHT BEFORE RESPONDING TO AN INSULT, WAIT 20 SECONDS BEFORE ANSWERING A SEEMINGLY STUPID QUESTION ABOUT YOUR PRESENTATION.

~ BE AS RESPECTFUL & FRIENDLY AS POSSIBLE TO EVERYONE YOU MEET. WE ALL BELONG TO THE SAME IN-GROUP, & THE JOURNEY AHEAD IS A DIFFICULT & DANGEROUS ONE FOR EVERY SINGLE ONE OF US. MAKE YOURSELF AWARE EVERY DAY OF THE SIMILARITIES YOU SHARE WITH ALL OTHER PEOPLE, & USE THEM AS A STARTING POINT FOR YOUR ACTIONS—AS WELL AS FOR YOUR PRESENTATIONS—INSTEAD OF CONCENTRATING ON THE DIFFERENCES. AVOID MASS EVENTS, BUT SEEK OCCASIONS FOR SPIRITUALLY BONDING WITH OTHER PEOPLE.

~ LIVE LIKE THE PEOPLE YOU ADMIRE MOST. LISTEN TO EVERYONE WITH PATIENCE, ENCOURAGE THEM, BE THE LOVING & CARING PERSON YOU MISSED SO MUCH IN YOUR OWN CHILDHOOD. HELP OTHERS TO LIVE HOPEFULLY, COURAGEOUSLY & WITH DIGNITY. BE A HERO, TRY TO LEAD AN EXTRAORDINARY & AUTHENTIC LIFE, DEFEND THE MANY, FIGHT PEACEFULLY AGAINST THE FEW.

~ TRY TO BE MORE GENEROUS EVERY DAY. GIVE AWAY THINGS & MONEY, GIVE SHELTER, INSPIRE THE PEOPLE AROUND YOU & MAKE COMPASSION & LOVE THE ULTIMATE GOALS OF YOUR LIFE.

~ WHEN A STRANGER IS PASSING YOU BY, THINK AT LEAST FIVE TIMES A DAY, "MAY YOU SUCCEED IN BECOMING FREE OF SUFFERING & PAIN, MAY YOU SUCCEED IN ATTAINING PEACE & HAPPINESS."

~ ALWAYS TRY TO SEE THE BEAUTY IN EVERYTHING THERE IS, BUT ALSO THE FRAGILITY THAT IS HIDDEN IN EVERYTHING THERE IS. BECOME AN AMBASSADOR OF BEAUTY, LOVE & COMPASSION. DON'T WAIT. LIFE IS SHORT. GO AHEAD.

~ TAKE RESPONSIBILITY. DEMOCRACY, JUSTICE & PEACE DEPEND ON YOUR DAILY DECISIONS AND ACTIONS. USE YOUR PRESENTATIONS TO INSPIRE OTHERS WITH YOUR VISION OF A BETTER FUTURE.

~ KEEP LOOKING AT THE STARS. CONNECT TO THE UNIVERSE. SWING, IF ONLY FOR A SECOND, IN HARMONY WITH THE LOVE THAT FILLS EVERYTHING AROUND YOU WITH ITS MELODY.

"THIS WORLD IS INDEED A LIVING BEING ENDOWED WITH A SOUL AND INTELLIGENCE, CONTAINING ALL OTHER LIVING ENTITIES, WHICH BY THEIR NATURE ARE ALL RELATED."

~ PLATO

As I write these lines here in my café opposite the university, our world seems to be in turmoil. Covid-19, an ongoing economic crisis and endless wars in the Middle East with millions of people living in refugee camps or fleeing have shaken our confidence in the future.

When I look at the world through the window of my regular café today, 24 July 2020, I actually have good reasons to be discouraged or even desperate. But I am not discouraged, and I am not desperate because I think I understand what is really going on.

THE MEDIA ARE FAILING IN THEIR TASK~

The media, which should explain to us what is happening in the world today, are unfortunately controlled by the Few, and the power of those Few is based on our feeling that the world economy and world politics are chaotic, uncontrollable and downward bound—and that everything we are seeing and experiencing is the result of a chain of tragic coincidences.

I am well aware of the fact that a global system consisting of almost 200 nations and over eight billion people does produce coincidences, but this does not mean that all mergers, regime changes and civil wars in this world are in fact coincidences.

I think that there are individuals in governments, political parties, media groups, intelligence services, companies, banks and think tanks who know each other, regularly exchange views and are responsible for much of what is happening in our world today.

This may sound like a big conspiracy theory to you—a term created by the CIA, by the way—and may elicit a compassionate smile from you, but is this idea really that absurd?

I find it interesting that a look at our recent history in Europe reveals a clear overarching military strategy behind many of the political events that were difficult to understand at the time.

The terrorist attacks in Italy during my childhood, the kidnapping and murder of the politician Aldo Moro, the Mafia attacks on judges and police officers—they were all part of a "strategia della tensione", a "strategy of tension", aimed at securing the economic, political and military domination of Europe by the United States.

This strategy was implemented through the cooperation of western intelligence services, masonic lodges, individual NATO military personnel, journalists and members of organised crime. Why should it be any different today?

The circles of power ~

Just ask yourself the mother of all questions: "Cui bono?"

Who benefits most from the wars in Syria and Libya, from refugee flows and terrorist attacks, from the weakness of the European economies and from the civil wars in the Middle East and in Africa?

Seneca gives us the answer: "Cui prodest scelus, is fecit". "Those who profit from a crime have committed it." Well, the list of profiteers is surprisingly short compared to the apparent complexity of our world today:

~ The military and the arms industry.
~ The big oil companies.
~ The secret services.
~ Organised crime.
~ The big banks.

Caution, most people who work in these organisations are not worse people than you and me, and many of them are not even aware of who they actually work for.

But in each of these organisations there are small circles that keep in touch with other circles of power, and I am convinced that these few hundreds of people are directly or indirectly responsible for 90% of all the criminal, terrorist and warlike acts we are witnessing worldwide today.

We must establish democratic control ~

In his epochal speech to the students of the American University in Washington on 10 June 1963, President John F. Kennedy said something that could serve as a beacon of light today, in a time that seems much darker than it actually is:

"Our problems are man-made, therefore they may be solved by man. And man can be as big as he wants. No problem of human destiny is beyond human beings."

If we succeed in bringing our armed forces, our oil companies, our secret services and above all our banks under democratic control, not only will organised crime suddenly lose a large part of its power, but 90% of all acts of war and terror will cease overnight. It's that simple, and it's that hard.

The CIA, the US Army, NATO, the oil companies and banks, the Bilderberger and the masonic lodges, all these organisations are originally useful institutions behind which a few conspirators are hiding today. But they can only do that until we, the Many, remind them again of the original social contract and curtail their life-threatening omnipotence.

The loving spirit who fills the whole universe will be with us and in us while we will undertake this difficult journey. The moment we become aware of our possibilities, we are filled with this loving power, and then no assassin, no TV-show and no cheque will be able to take away the certainty from us that the supreme being, the universe and Gaia, our Mother Earth, will always be on our side.

It's time we become aware of our power ~

We need to change our way of thinking about ourselves and the world. Our most important task today is not solving problems but anticipating a new world and a new way to live in our minds.

The creativity, courage and energy we need to save our world are already within us, just waiting to be liberated. Our stories, songs and poems are already more powerful than the greed, the lies and the violence of the Few. We, the Many, are the United Nations, we, the Many, are the United Religions, we, the Many, are the United Capitalists as well as the United Anti-Capitalists, the United Workers as well as the United Entrepreneurs.

The future demands from us that we, the Many, join forces in a common, powerful, yet truly democratic vision.

Once we will have achieved this, most of the problems that still seem insurmountable to us today will be solved forever and for the benefit of all living beings.

Conscious in our power and united in respect and compassion, we will create a new world.

I VOW TO ADDRESS THIS TO-DO-LIST FOR THE 21ST CENTURY WITH MY PRESENTATIONS:

~ I WILL DO MY BEST TO BECOME AWARE AND TO HELP OTHERS TO BECOME AWARE AND TO GROW. I WILL EMBRACE NATURE, MEDITATION AND THE SEARCH FOR REAL LOVE.

~ I WILL HELP TO CREATE A NEW, POSITIVE ECONOMY BASED ON LONG-TERM BENEFITS FOR ALL.

~ I WILL HELP TO REDUCE THE PRIVILEGES OF THE FEW —IN BANKS, BIG CORPORATIONS AND MASONIC LODGES—AND THEIR INFLUENCE ON POLITICS AND THE MEDIA.

~ I WILL HELP TO FIGHT INEQUALITY IN THE DISTRIBUTION OF WATER, FOOD, INCOME, EDUCATION AND MEANS OF COMMUNICATION GLOBALLY, AND I WILL DONATE MONEY AND TIME TO CHARITY.

~ I WILL HELP TO PREVENT TOTAL CONTROL OF OUR PRIVACY, OF POLITICS AND OF THE INTERNET BY THE GOVERNMENTS, THE INTERNATIONAL CORPORATIONS AND THE SECRET AGENCIES.

~ I WILL SUSTAIN THE FIGHT FOR HUMAN RIGHTS OF WORKERS, CHILDREN, WOMEN AND MINORITIES, WHERE I LIVE AS WELL AS ON THE INTERNET.

~ I WILL HELP TO ESTABLISH CLOSED PRODUCTION-RECYCLING-CYCLES AND FIND SOLUTIONS FOR THE DETOXIFICATION OF THE ENVIRONMENT. I WILL REDUCE MY OWN CONSUMPTION AND WASTE.

~ I WILL HELP TO TURN AROUND GLOBAL WARMING, AND I WILL REDUCE MY OWN CO_2-IMPRINT.

~ I WILL HELP TO PRESERVE THE BEAUTIFUL BIODIVERSITY OF OUR PLANET.

~ I WILL HELP TO END THE ARMS RACE AND ASK MY GOVERNMENT TO STOP SELLING WEAPONS OF ANY KIND.

"THREE THINGS HAVE REMAINED OF PARADISE: THE STARS OF THE NIGHT, THE FLOWERS OF THE DAY AND THE EYES OF THE CHILDREN."

~ DANTE ALIGHIERI

The greatness and future of a man lies not in his material wealth, the greatness and future of a company cannot be expressed by measuring its profit and the greatness and future of a nation cannot be described by calculating its gross national product.

TRUE GREATNESS CREATES VALUE FOR ALL ~

A person's greatness and future lies in his ability to become conscious, to help others and to change the world for the better. Great women and men strive to give away more and more of themselves and of what they possess throughout their lives.

The greatness and future of a company lies in its ability to look after all stake-holders: great companies respect and value their customers at a fair price, treat their employees with respect, protect and enrich the cities and countries in which they operate and are committed to a green planet and a fairer world.

They return more value to our planet than they take from it, as Tony Schwartz once so aptly put it.

The greatness and future of a nation lies in its ability to create prosperity and happiness for the greatest possible number of citizens, and not just for a few. A nation's wealth and future lies in an excellent education for all, in functioning infrastructures, in a functioning health care for all, in environmentally friendly, affordable and decentralised energy and in a green environment in general.

A great nation is a place with a future where "every life can be truly and completely lived", as Umair Haque so brilliantly puts it in his blog about the US-society.

A NATION WITH A FEW TECHNOLOGY COMPANIES THAT PRODUCE MILLIONS OF APPS BUT ONLY A FEW DOZEN JOBS IS NOT A GREAT NATION AND HAS NO FUTURE.

A NATION THAT SUFFOCATES DISSATISFACTION WITH POLICEMEN AND SOLDIERS IN ITS OWN COUNTRY WHILE INSTIGATING CIVIL WARS AND STEALING RESOURCES ABROAD IS NOT A GREAT NATION AND HAS NO FUTURE.

A NATION IN WHICH 1% OF THE POPULATION CONTROLS TWO THIRDS OF ALL WEALTH IS NOT A GREAT NATION AND HAS NO FUTURE.

DO YOU LIVE IN A GREAT NATION? ~

THAT IS WHY TODAY, ON THIS WARM DAY IN JULY 2020, I AM MORE CONVINCED THAN EVER THAT WE MUST DEVELOP A NEW VISION OF A DESIRABLE FUTURE FOR US ALL. FOR ME, THE GROUND PLAN OF THIS VISION CONSISTS IN A FEW IDEAS:

~ MULTINATIONALS ARE TOO POWERFUL TODAY, AND THEY INFLUENCE THE ECONOMY, POLITICS AND THE MASS MEDIA MORE THAN IS GOOD FOR US. WE MUST GET THEM TO PAY MORE TAXES, AND WE MUST FIND WAYS TO HELP THEM PROTECT THE INTERESTS OF THE MANY FROM THE GREED OF A FEW SHAREHOLDERS.

~ WE MUST FIGHT INEQUALITY AT GLOBAL LEVEL, WE MUST CLOSE THE ENORMOUS GAP BETWEEN BILLIONS OF POOR PEOPLE ON THE ONE HAND AND A FEW SUPER-RICH ON THE OTHER.

~ WE MUST REDUCE THE NUMBER OF SECRET SERVICES AND MASONIC LODGES AROUND THE WORLD, AND WE MUST BRING THEM UNDER TRULY DEMOCRATIC CONTROL. THE SAME APPLIES TO THE WEAPON INDUSTRY, THE BIG BANKS AND ORGANISED CRIME. THESE MOSTLY UNCONTROLLED POWER CIRCLES HAVE CREATED A NETWORK OF VERY DANGEROUS RELATIONS WHICH WE MUST BREAK UP IF THE TERM "DEMOCRACY" IS TO BE MORE THAN JUST A LABEL FOR A DE FACTO DICTATORSHIP.

~ WE MUST OPPOSE ANY KIND OF RELIGIOUS FANATICISM, STARTING WITH OUR OWN RELIGIONS. RELIGIONS MUST BECOME UNIFYING FORCES AGAIN, ABOVE ALL THROUGH THE TEACHING OF TOLERANCE AND COMPASSION, OTHERWISE THEY LOSE THEIR ORIGINAL MEANING.

~ WE MUST TEACH OUR CHILDREN THAT ANIMALS, PLANTS AND TREES ALSO POSSESS AWARENESS AND ALSO DO HAVE SOULS, AND THAT, CONSEQUENTLY, THEIR LIVES ARE SACRED AND WORTH PROTECTING AND MUST NOT BE SACRIFICED TO THE ABSURD GREED FOR FLESH.

~ CULTURE MUST REGAIN PRIMACY OVER TECHNOLOGY, OTHERWISE WE RISK CREATING A CIVILISATION OF SMARTPHONE IDIOTS WITHOUT ANY IDEA OF LOVE, COMPASSION AND TOLERANCE.

~ BUT ABOVE ALL: POLITICS MUST ONCE AGAIN BECOME A SOURCE OF VISIONS, INSTEAD OF CONTINUING TO BE A BLACK BOX FOR THE UNJUST DISTRIBUTION OF SOCIAL WEALTH. SINCE THE BEGINNING OF TIME, OUR WORLD HAS ALWAYS BEEN TRANSFORMED BY VISIONS AND THE POSSIBILITY OF DISCUSSING THESE VISIONS FREELY.

WE MUST SAVE OUR FUTURE ~

OUR WORLD, OUR NATIONS, OUR CORPORATIONS AND OURSELVES ARE OUT OF BALANCE, AND NO POLITICIAN, GURU OR COMIC BOOK SUPERHERO CAN SOLVE THIS PROBLEM FOR US —WE MUST DO IT OURSELVES.

IF WE DO NOT MANAGE TO UNITE ALL TOGETHER INTO A GLITTERING WAVE OF TRANSFORMATION, WE WILL NOT ONLY KILL OURSELVES AND THE PEOPLE WE LOVE BUT ALSO ALL FUTURE GENERATIONS WHO, STILL UNBORN, ARE DEPENDENT ON OUR ABILITY TO DEAL WISELY WITH THE PRESENT.

EXCERPT FROM THE CAMBRIDGE DECLARATION OF CONSCIOUSNESS, 2012:

"WE DECLARE THE FOLLOWING: THE ABSENCE OF A NEOCORTEX DOES NOT APPEAR TO PRECLUDE AN ORGANISM FROM EXPERIENCING AFFECTIVE STATES.

CONVERGENT EVIDENCE INDICATES THAT NON-HUMAN ANIMALS HAVE THE NEUROANATOMICAL, NEUROCHEMICAL & NEUROPHYSIOLOGICAL SUBSTRATES OF CONSCIOUS STATES ALONG WITH THE CAPACITY TO EXHIBIT INTENTIONAL BEHAVIOURS.

CONSEQUENTLY, THE WEIGHT OF EVIDENCE INDICATES THAT HUMANS ARE NOT UNIQUE IN POSSESSING THE NEUROLOGICAL SUBSTRATES THAT GENERATE CONSCIOUSNESS.

NON-HUMAN ANIMALS, INCLUDING ALL MAMMALS & BIRDS, & MANY OTHER CREATURES, INCLUDING OCTOPUSES, ALSO POSSESS THESE NEUROLOGICAL SUBSTRATES."

Arrivederci! ~
Together we will transform the world

"Though no one can go back and make a brand new start, anyone can start from now and make a brand new ending."

~ Carl Bard

I am sure that we humans can achieve everything we want. We can be rational and spiritual beings, intelligent and visionary beings, successful and compassionate beings at the same time and overcome every limit, every obstacle and even death.

The highest being is in each of us, and each of us is a piece of him, of her, of it—and thus divine. That means that every transformation in a single human being changes the whole universe and every other living being in it. We are all part of the same immense holography, the same immortal consciousness, the same boundless love that has never begun and will never end.

This book was about you ~

Therefore, although it was me writing it, this book was not about me, it was about you. I'm you. You wrote this book, and I'm reading it now. You are me. That's why the revolution always begins where you are right now, where I am right now, where our brothers and sisters are right now.

The revolution is everywhere—if enough of us start their transformation at the same time.

Therefore, please, spread the wings of your imagination, and do it now, or your children's children will inherit a world from you where nobody dreams anymore. So, please, learn to get by with less things today, or your children's children will be buried in garbage cemeteries. So, please, face the Few bravely in your days to come, or your children's children will be slaves all their lives.

I believe in you ~

Although I don't know you, I believe in you. Do you know why? Because I know that deep down in our hearts, we are all connected, and that we all dream the same dream. You're us, and we're you.

That's why I'm looking forward to your presentations because I know that from today on you will not only inform your listeners but also touch them and shake them up.

That's why I look forward to your presentations because I know that from today on you will go far beyond the four horizons of your slides and show us a way into the future instead of just numbers, charts and prizes.

That's why I look forward to your presentations because the moment you will really become aware of your possibilities, your presentations will be as inspiring as you are.

Let's live a great life! ~

My friend, my brother, my sister: live and enjoy your life, and reserve a corner of your heart for me and for all the other beings who live with you on this planet today.

Our life will be great. You know why I say that? Because I believe in us. Because I believe in the great, beautiful wave of transformation that is building right now. Because I believe that from tomorrow on, we are all destined to live in a fairer, more peaceful and truly human world.

Marina di Massa, 24 July 2015–Mannheim, 24 July 2020

I WOULD LIKE TO THANK FROM THE HEART:

MARCELLA LALLI GALLINI
LUCIO LALLI
BARBARA LALLI
MARCO LALLI
OSCAR LALLI
LAURA CANCELLI GALLINI
GIUSEPPE CANCELLI
GIORGIO GALLINI
CARLO GALLINI
PAOLA PIERACCI GALLINI
ELISA GALLINI
LORENZO GALLINI
MICHELA TARABELLA PAPUCCI
MAURIZIO PAPUCCI
VALERIA LALLI ZANNI

&

MONIKA
SANDRA
MELISSA
JULIE
KATJA
ANNIKA

"THROUGH LOVE, ALL THAT IS BITTER NOW WILL BECOME SWEET. THROUGH LOVE, ALL THAT IS STILL COPPER WILL TURN INTO GOLD. THROUGH LOVE, ALL THAT IS STILL SEDIMENT WILL TURN INTO WINE. THROUGH LOVE, ALL THAT IS STILL HURTING WILL TURN INTO MEDICINE."

~ RUMI